THE RENAISSANCE BAZAAR

THE RENAISSANCE BAZAAR
From the Silk Road to Michelangelo

Jerry Brotton

OXFORD
UNIVERSITY PRESS

OXFORD
UNIVERSITY PRESS

Great Clarendon Street, Oxford ox2 6dp

Oxford University Press is a department of the University of Oxford.
It furthers the University's objective of excellence in research, scholarship,
and education by publishing worldwide in

Oxford New York

Auckland Bangkok Buenos Aires Cape Town Chennai
Dar es Salaam Delhi Hong Kong Istanbul Karachi Kolkata
Kuala Lumpur Madrid Melbourne Mexico City Mumbai Nairobi
São Paulo Shanghai Singapore Taipei Tokyo Toronto

with an associated company in Berlin

Oxford is a registered trade mark of Oxford University Press
in the UK and in certain other countries

Published in the United States
by Oxford University Press Inc., New York

British Library Cataloguing in Publication Data

Data available

Library of Congress Cataloging in Publication Data

Data available

ISBN 0–19–280268–2

1 3 5 7 9 10 8 6 4 2

Typeset in Scala
by RefineCatch Limited, Bungay, Suffolk
Printed in Spain by Book Print S. L.

CONTENTS

PREFACE

If there is one moment at which most people define the birth of modern European civilization, it is surely the period between 1400 and 1600 known as the Renaissance. *The Renaissance Bazaar* argues that modern Europe emerged in this period by competing and exchanging ideas and commodities with its eastern (and predominantly Islamic) neighbours. These east–west transactions laid the bases for the great art and culture that we now associate with the Renaissance. They also reveal that Europe emerged in close relation rather than stark opposition to the cultures and communities it has often come to demonize and label as underdeveloped and uncivilized.

Scholars across the humanities are already developing this approach to the Renaissance. However, *The Renaissance Bazaar* is the first book to synthesize these developments, and suggest how an understanding of the impact of the east transforms our understanding of the Renaissance. My own collaborative work with Lisa Jardine, alongside the writings of scholars like Gülru Necipoğlu, Nabil Matar, Joan Pau Rubiés, Deborah Howard, and Julian Raby, has started to reconsider the ways in which the Renaissance looks very different when viewed from beyond the bounds of Europe. Rather than signalling an end to the study of the Renaissance, this book suggests that exciting discoveries still lie ahead.

I would like to thank Matt Birchwood, Mat Dimmock, Margaret Ferguson, Don and Sarah Holmes, Adam Lowe, Karin Pibernik, Evelyn Welch, and, at Oxford, Ali Chivers for their help and suggestions in the completion of this book. No one could wish for a better mentor and collaborator than Lisa Jardine. She

was instrumental in encouraging me to write this book, and per-
sistently prevented me from being hypnotized by the seductive
myths of the Renaissance with her characteristic verve and
ingenuity. I look forward to further collaborations and voyages of
discovery with her on an even grander scale.

This book is dedicated to my most sceptical critic, Rachel
Holmes. She has read every page, questioned every assumption,
and demanded clarity at every point. The result is a much better
book than I could have written without her, although any mistakes and omissions remain my own. I hope that she now agrees
with me that the Renaissance is worth the effort.

LIST OF PLATES

1 Hans Holbein, the Younger, *The Ambassadors*, 1533, oil on canvas, National Gallery, London.

2 Gentile Bellini (attributed), *The Sultan Mehmed II*, c.1479, oil on canvas, National Gallery, London.

3 Abraham Cresques, detail of North Africa, first two panels of *The Catalan Atlas*, 1375, vellum on wood, Bibliothèque Nationale, Paris / The Bridgeman Art Library.

4 'Aristotle and Averroës' by Girolams da Cremona, from Aristotle, *Works*, print and paint, vol. I, 1483, Venice. Pierpoint Morgan Library, New York, PML21194, folio 2r. / Art Resource, New York.

5 Raphael's workshop, *Donation of Constantine*, 1523–4, fresco, north wall, Sala di Constantino, Vatican / Scala.

6 Fra Angelico, *Linaiuoli Altarpiece*, 1433, tempera on panel, Museo di San Marco, Florence / Scala.

7 Costanzo da Ferrara, *Seated Scribe*, c.1470–80, pen and gouache, Isabella Stewart Gardner Museum, Boston / The Bridgeman Art Library.

8 Bihzād, *Portrait of a Painter*, late 15th century, Freer Gallery of Art, Smithsonian, Washington DC.: purchase, F1932.28.

LIST OF ILLUSTRATIONS

INTRODUCTION

The Renaissance Bazaar describes the historical period starting in the early 15th century when eastern and western societies vigorously traded art, ideas, and luxury goods in a competitive but amicable exchange that shaped what we now call the European Renaissance. The eastern bazaar is a fitting metaphor for the fluid transactions that occurred throughout the 15th and 16th centuries, when Europe began to define itself by purchasing and emulating the opulence and cultured sophistication of the cities, merchants, scholars, and empires of the Ottomans, the Persians and the Egyptian Mamluks. The flow of spices, silks, carpets, porcelain, majolica, porphyry, glassware, lacquer, dyes, and pigments from the eastern bazaars of Muslim Spain, Mamluk Egypt, Ottoman Turkey, Persia, and the Silk Road between China and Europe provided the inspiration and materials for the art and architecture of Bellini, van Eyck, Dürer, and Alberti. The transmission of Arabic understanding of astronomy, philosophy, and medicine also profoundly influenced thinkers and scientists like Leonardo da Vinci, Copernicus, Vesalius, and Montaigne, whose insights into the workings of the human mind and body, as well as the individual's relationship to the wider world, are often still seen as the foundation of modern science and philosophy. It was the complex impact of these exchanges between east and west that created the culture, art, and scholarship that have been popularly associated with the Renaissance.

Since the 11th-, 12th-, and 13th-century European Crusades in the Holy Land, Christians and Muslims had openly traded and exchanged goods and ideas despite religious antagonism and military conflict. Towards the end of the 13th century the Venetian merchant Marco Polo had gone even further, travelling as far as China in search of new commercial possibilities. By the 14th century, the political and commercial worlds of both Europe and Asia were undergoing profound changes. Europe found itself trading on equal terms with powerful empires in Egypt, Persia, and Turkey. Two examples of these exchanges set the tone of this book, and capture the impact of the east upon 15th- and 16th-century Europe. In 1487 the Egyptian Mamluk Sultan Qā'it Bāy sent a magnificent embassy to Florence in an attempt to establish a commercial agreement intended to cut the rival Ottoman Empire out of the Italian trade. The secretary to Florence's ruler Lorenzo de' Medici recalled with astonishment that the Egyptian retinue arrived with riches rarely seen in Italy. These included balsam, musk, benzoin, aloeswood, ginger, muslin, thorough-bred Arabian horses, and Chinese porcelain. The impact of these luxurious objects upon Italian life was recorded in the paintings and architectural details of Masaccio, Filarete, and Mantegna, who all incorporated exotic animals, Islamic script, and the lustre of lacquered wood, porphyry, patterned silk, and intricately designed carpets into their paintings. Leonardo had already been so impressed by Qā'it Bāy's reputation that in 1484 he wrote a series of reports to 'Kait-Bai' on scientific and architectural initiatives he proposed to undertake in Turkey. Leonardo clearly believed that wealth, patronage, and political power lay in the courts to the east of mainland Europe.

Nearly a century later, a very different exchange took place, this time from the west to the east. In 1578 Queen Elizabeth I of England sent a consignment of goods including lead for the production of armaments to Sultan Murat III in Istanbul. Having been excommunicated by the Pope eight years earlier, Elizabeth had no scruples about agreeing to England's status as a vassal state of the Ottoman Empire to stimulate trade and woo the Ottomans as potential allies against Catholic Spain. England's surprising alliance with the Ottomans had a direct impact upon the drama and literature of Elizabethan England, including Christopher Marlowe's plays *Tamburlaine the Great* (1587) and *The Jew of Malta* (1590) and Shakespeare's *Othello, the Moor of Venice* (1603). Both these examples show that some of the greatest products of European Renaissance culture emerged from encounters and exchanges with the east. Although Europe was publicly committed to military conflict and opposition to the Islamic empires on its eastern borders, trade and exchange usually continued regardless of ideological differences.

These stories are just part of a larger body of evidence that confounds an increasingly moribund version of the Renaissance. This account claims that from the late 14th century, European culture rediscovered a lost Graeco-Roman intellectual tradition that allowed scholars and artists based almost exclusively in Italy to develop more cultured and civilized ways of thinking and acting. This in turn created the conditions for the literature, art, and philosophy of the likes of Petrarch, Michelangelo, and Ficino. This approach also argued that the Renaissance formed the enduring basis of modern European civilization.

This book suggests that once we begin to understand the impact of eastern cultures upon mainland Europe *c.*1400–1600, then this traditional understanding of the European Renaissance collapses. It also suggests that there is no one single, unified theory or vision of the European Renaissance. The impact of the east had a decisive effect upon the outlook of mainland Europe by the 16th century, but there were other factors that also changed European society within this period. The invention of printing in Germany in the mid-15th century and Luther's Reformation in the early 16th century were not influenced by the same factors that inspired the Italian art of Bellini and Mantegna. In many respects these northern European developments were deeply hostile to the art, philosophy, and political culture of Italy that is usually perceived to be quintessentially 'Renaissance'. The late 15th-century Iberian voyages of discovery produced cultures in Portugal and Castile that had little in common with what was happening in Germany or Italy. Profound regional differences in politics, art, and society suggest that it has become impossible to sustain a belief in one coherent attitude or 'spirit' driving forward the European Renaissance.

However, *The Renaissance Bazaar* is not aimed at simply taking apart the myth of the European Renaissance. While the book is sceptical about the validity of the grand claims to European superiority often associated with the celebration of the Renaissance, it argues that an appreciation of regional differences and the impact of the east enables scholars and readers to discover an even more exciting moment in European history, which allows different cultures into the picture. One of the arguments of this book is that every generation creates a version of the European Renaissance in its own image. In this respect, *The Renaissance Bazaar* is no different. In a global climate where the dangers of political and religious fundamentalism jostle with renewed possibilities for cultural exchange and cooperation, it is time to look at the period known as the Renaissance as a moment that similarly stood on the threshold of an expanding world where people exchanged ideas and things often regardless of political and religious ideology.

The vast literature on the subject means that *The Renaissance Bazaar* offers a considered and selective account of the Renaissance, much of which will be familiar to general readers, but some of which will hopefully be new and surprising. As the book's title suggests, trade and exchange with the east is a dominating motif: this forms the basis of the first chapter, which draws on Europe's encounters and exchanges with the Ottoman Empire, Africa, and Southeast Asia to offer a more global perspective on the period. In the Renaissance bazaar different cultures confronted each other with bewilderment and suspicion, but often delight and fascination as well. They exchanged objects and ideas that went against religious and political proscriptions that stressed cultural separation and mutual antagonism.

In trying to understand how the idea of the Renaissance has evolved, the book begins with a critical history of the evolution of the term. Having established the shape and scope of the Renaissance, it then looks more closely at interactions between east and west throughout the 15th and 16th centuries. It goes on to examine what has been considered one of the most important, but also controversial achievements of the Renaissance: the scholarly practice of humanism. The focus then broadens again to explore the religious and political conflicts that defined the period, from the papal schism in Italy in the late 13th century to the northern European Reformation of the 16th century and the part that the Ottoman Empire played in the imperial conflicts of the time. Chapter 4 surveys general developments in art and architecture, before examining more specifically east–west artistic exchanges, and the centrality of art and building in the creation of political power. Central to any discussion of the Renaissance is the so-called Age of Discovery, the great overseas voyages of Columbus, da Gama, and Magellan that took place between 1480 and 1540. The penultimate chapter explores these voyages in the light of the desire to reach the markets of the east, and follows their development and consequences through the rise of maps and charts. Finally, the book addresses developments in 15th- and early 16th-century science and philosophy, and the ways in which their insights were developed in literature from Dante to Shakespeare.

This book does not claim to offer a comprehensive survey of the Renaissance. There is little here on antiquity, music, law, witchcraft, and rural life. To cover every possible historical topic is not only impossible, but runs the risk of turning the book into a social history of Europe between 1400 and 1600. The idea of the Renaissance is an elite concept, based on the cultural ideals of a very small stratum of society. While this book aims to broaden the focus and include figures usually marginalized in traditional accounts of the Renaissance, any understanding of the concept involves an examination of its established cultural brokers, from Leonardo and Machiavelli to Luther and Shakespeare. The book begins by explaining both traditional and alternative perspectives on the Renaissance through an examination of one of its most iconic images: Hans Holbein's painting *The Ambassadors*.

An Old Master

In 1997 the National Gallery in London launched an exhibition entitled 'Making and Meaning' based exclusively on one of the most famous works of art in its collection—Holbein's *The Ambassadors*, dated 1533 (Plate 1). The success of the exhibition was due to the fact that for many people Holbein's painting is an abiding image of the European Renaissance. To visit an exhibition that promised to unravel the painting's mysteries, its innovative composition, the identity of its two central figures, and the meaning of its various artefacts, was to begin to understand the very idea of 'the Renaissance'. In what follows, I use this painting to define the broad outlines of the Renaissance, touching on some of the key ideas and concepts that are central to an understanding of what is meant when this contentious term is used.

What is it that makes Holbein's painting so quintessentially 'Renaissance'? To begin with, its medium represents for many people the most enduring dimension of the Renaissance: the painting of artists like Botticelli, Dürer, Leonardo, and Michelangelo. Traditionally, critics have argued that the Renaissance is defined by the birth of a modern type of individuality, or what the 19th-century historian Jules Michelet called 'the discovery of the world and of man'. According to this argument, from the 14th century onwards an increasingly enquiring, psychological, and reflective form of personal individuality emerged, that began to question and explore what it means to be human and the place of humanity within a wider world. The supreme manifestation of this development is the art of the period that culminated in the paintings of artists like Holbein. In *The Ambassadors* can be seen the detailed, precise reproduction of the world of two Renaissance men, who stare back at the viewer with a confident, but also questioning self-awareness that has arguably not been seen before in painting. Medieval art may seem much more alien, as it lacks this powerfully self-conscious creation of individuality. Even if it is difficult to grasp the motivation for the range of emotions expressed in paintings like Holbein's, it is still possible to identify with these emotions as recognizably 'modern'. In other words, when we look at paintings like *The Ambassadors*, we are witnessing the birth of modern man.

This is a useful start in trying to understand Holbein's painting as an artistic manifestation of the Renaissance. But some rather vague terms are beginning to accumulate that need some explanation. What is the 'modern world'? Isn't this as slippery a term as 'Renaissance'? Similarly, should medieval art be defined (and effectively dismissed) so simply? And what of 'Renaissance Man'? Is it feasible to talk about 'Renaissance Woman'? Holbein's painting can be used to explore a whole different set of ideas about what characterized the Renaissance and which will form the basis for many of the discussions in this book.

An educated Renaissance

In the painting what catches the eye as much as the gaze of both sitters is the table in the middle of the composition and the objects scattered across its upper and lower tiers. On the lower shelf are two books (a hymn book and a merchant's arithmetic book), a lute, a terrestrial globe, a case of flutes, a set square, and a pair of dividers. The upper shelf contains a celestial globe, and several extremely specialized scientific instruments: quadrants, sundials, and a torquetum (a timepiece and navigational aid). These objects represent the seven liberal arts that provided the basis of a Renaissance education. The three basic arts—grammar, logic, and rhetoric—were known as the *trivium*. They can be loosely related to the display of books and the activities of the two sitters. They are ambassadors, trained in the use of texts, but above all skilled in the art of logical argument and rhetorical persuasion. The *quadrivium* referred to arithmetic, music, geometry, and astronomy, all of which are clearly represented in Holbein's precise depiction of the arithmetic book, the lute, and the scientific instruments.

These academic subjects formed the basis of the *studia humanitatis*, the course of study followed by most young men of the period. This was the basis of what has become known as humanism. Humanism represented a significant new development in late 14th- and 15th-century Europe that involved the recovery of the classical texts of Greek and Roman language, culture, politics, and philosophy. The highly flexible nature of the *studia humanitatis* encouraged the study of a variety of new disciplines, such as classical philology, literature, history, and moral philosophy.

Holbein is showing that his sitters are themselves 'New Men', scholarly, worldly figures, utilizing their learning in pursuit of fame and ambition. The figure on the right is Jean de Dinteville, the French ambassador to the English court of Henry VIII. On the left is his close friend Georges de Selve, Bishop of Lavaur, who visited Dinteville in London in 1533. The objects on the table are carefully chosen to suggest that their position in the worlds of politics and religion are closely connected to their understanding of humanist thinking. The painting implies that knowledge of the disciplines represented by these objects is crucial to worldly ambition and success.

The darker side of the Renaissance

If we look even more closely at the objects in Holbein's painting, they lead us into a darker and less familiar vision of the Renaissance. Consider the objects portrayed on the lower shelf. One of the strings on the lute is broken, a deliberate symbol of discord. Next to the lute is an open hymn book, identifiable as the work of the great religious reformer Martin Luther. On the very right-hand edge of the painting, the curtain is slightly pulled back to reveal a silver crucifix. These objects draw our attention to the pervasive importance of religious debate and discord in the Renaissance. At the time the painting was commissioned, Luther's Protestant ideas were sweeping through Europe, defying the established authority of the Roman Catholic Church. The broken lute is a powerful symbol of the religious conflict that characterized the Renaissance period, graphically captured by Holbein in his juxtaposition of Lutheran hymn book and Catholic crucifix.

Holbein's Lutheran hymn book is quite clearly a printed book. The invention of printing in the latter half of the 15th century revolutionized the creation, distribution, and understanding of information and knowledge. Compared to the laborious and often inaccurate copying of manuscripts, printed books could be circulated with a speed and accuracy and in quantities previously unimaginable. Luther's radical new ideas would have foundered without the aid of the printing press. However, as Luther's example also suggests, many of the greatest cultural and techno-logical achievements of the Renaissance provoked instability, uncertainty, and anxiety, and the ethos of the period can be defined as struggling with this dilemma.

Next to Holbein's Lutheran hymn book sits another printed book, which at first seems more mundane, but which offers another telling dimension of the Renaissance. The book is an instruction manual for merchants in how to calculate profit and loss. Its presence alongside the more 'cultural' objects in the painting shows that the Renaissance was itself as much about business and finance as culture and art. While the book alludes to the *quadrivium* of Renaissance humanist learning, it also points towards an awareness that the cultural achievements of the Renaissance were invariably built on the success of the spheres of trade and finance. As the world grew in size and complexity, new mechanisms for understanding the increasingly invisible circulation of money and goods were required to maximize profit and minimize loss. The result was a renewed interest in disciplines like mathematics as a way of understanding the economics of a progressively global Renaissance world picture.

The terrestrial globe behind the merchant's arithmetic book confirms the expansion of trade and finance as a defining feature of the Renaissance. The globe is one of the most important objects in the painting, both for Holbein's apprehension about his own time and our own contemporary understanding of why the Renaissance remains important today. Travel, exploration, and discovery were dynamic and controversial features during the Renaissance, and Holbein's globe tells us this in its remarkably up-to-date representation of the world as it was perceived in 1533. Europe is labelled 'Europa'. This is itself significant, as the 15th and 16th centuries were the point at which Europe began to be defined as possessing a common political and cultural identity. Prior to this people rarely called themselves 'European'. Holbein also portrays the recent discoveries made through voyages in Africa and Asia, as well as in the 'New World' voyages of Christopher Columbus, begun in 1492, and on the first ever circumnavigation of the globe, successfully completed by Ferdinand Magellan's expedition in 1522. These discoveries transformed Europe's understanding of its place in a world that was bigger than had previously been believed. With such discoveries came encounters and exchanges with other cultures whose complex legacy still remains today.

As with the impact of the printing press, and the upheavals in religion, this global expansion bequeathed a double-edged legacy. One of the outcomes was the destruction of indigenous cultures and communities through war and disease, because they were unprepared for or uninterested in adopting European beliefs and ways of living. As some critics argue, Columbus did not 'discover' America—he invaded it. Along with the cultural, scientific, and technological achievements of the period came religious intolerance, political ignorance, slavery, and massive inequalities in wealth and status—what has been called 'the darker side of the Renaissance'.

Politics and empire

This leads to other crucial dimensions of the Renaissance addressed in Holbein's painting, and which define both its sitters and the objects: power, politics, and empire. To understand the importance of these issues and how they emerge in the painting, we need to know some more about its subjects. In January 1533 King Henry VIII had secretly married Anne Boleyn and was pressing the pope for a divorce from his first wife. The pope refused. The French King Francis I negotiated between Henry and the pope in a vain attempt to prevent Henry's decision to split with Rome, and form the independent Church of England. Dinteville and Selve were there to act as Francis's intermediaries in these negotiations. While this painting, like much of the history of the Renaissance, is very much about relations between men, it is noticeable that at the heart of this image is a dispute over a woman who is absent, but whose presence is powerfully felt in its objects and surroundings. The insistent attempts by men to silence women only drew more attention to their complicated status within a patriarchal society: women were denied the benefits of many of the cultural and social developments of the Renaissance, but were key to its functioning as the bearers of male heirs to perpetuate its male-dominated culture.

It has often been thought that the primary motivation for the painting was the religious crisis of Henry's imminent split with Rome. But Dinteville and Selve were also in London to broker a new political alliance between Henry, Francis, and the Ottoman Sultan Süleyman the Magnificent, the other great power in European power politics of the time. The sumptuous rug that covers the upper shelf of the table in Holbein's painting is of Turkish design and manufacture, emphasizing that the Ottomans and their territories to the east were also part of the cultural, commercial, and political landscape of the Renaissance. Selve and Dinteville's attempt to draw Henry VIII into an alliance with Francis and Süleyman was motivated by their fear of the growing strength of that other great Renaissance imperial power, the Hapsburg empire of Charles V. By comparison England and France were eager but minor imperial players: the terrestrial globe in the painting says as much. It shows the European empires beginning to carve up the newly discovered world.

Holbein's globe reproduces the line of demarcation established by the empires of Spain and Portugal in 1494, in the aftermath of Columbus' 'discovery' of America in 1492. With the agreement of the pope, they divided up the globe by splitting it right down the middle. Portugal claimed all undiscovered lands to the east of the Atlantic, while Spain claimed everything to the west.

This division was made in response to a dispute over territories in the Far East. Both Spain and Portugal were struggling for possession of the remote but highly lucrative spice-producing islands of the Indonesian Archipelago, the Moluccas. In the Renaissance, Europe placed itself at the centre of the terrestrial globe, but its gaze was focused on the wealth of the east, from the textiles and silks of the Ottoman Empire to the spices and pepper of the Indonesian Archipelago. Many of the objects in Holbein's painting have an eastern origin, from the silk and velvet worn by its subjects to the textiles and designs that decorate the room. The painting is a triumphant image of northern European power, but it is also a magnificent display of the desire for and acquisition of eastern luxury that reached Europe via the Silk Road and the bazaars of Central Asia and the Far East.

The objects in the bottom section of Holbein's painting reveal various facets of the Renaissance central to the argument of this book—humanism and learning, religion, printing, trade, travel and exploration, politics and empire, and the enduring presence of the wealth and knowledge of the east. The objects on the upper shelf deal with much more abstract and philosophical issues. The celestial globe is an astronomical instrument used to measure the stars and the nature of the universe. Next to the globe is a collection of dials, which were used to tell the time with the aid of the sun's rays. The two larger objects are a quadrant and a torquetum, both used at sea as navigational instruments to work out a ship's position in both time and space. Most of these instruments were invented by medieval Arab and Jewish astronomers and came westwards as European travellers required navigational expertise for long-distance voyages. They reflect an intensified interest within the Renaissance to understand and master the natural world. As Renaissance philosophers debated the nature of their world, navigators, instrument-makers, and scientists began to channel these philosophical debates into practical solutions to natural problems. The results were objects such as those in Holbein's painting. In addition, there were other equally profound developments in areas such as firearms and ballistics, mechanics, shipbuilding, mining, distillation, and anatomy, to name but a few.

Finally, consider the strange, oblique image that slashes across the bottom of the painting. Viewed straight on, it is impossible to make out the meaning of this distorted shape. However, if the viewer stands at an angle to the painting, the distorted image metamorphoses into a perfectly drawn skull. This was a fashionable perspective trick known as anamorphosis used by several Renaissance artists, but nowhere more brilliantly than in Holbein's painting. Art historians have argued that this is a *vanitas* image, a chilling reminder that in the midst of all this wealth, power, and learning, death comes to us all. But the skull also appears to represent Holbein's own artistic initiative, regardless of the requirements of his patron. He begins to break free of his identity as skilled artisan and asserts the growing power and autonomy of the painter as an artist to experiment with new techniques and theories such as optics and geometry in creating innovative painted images. This development, glimpsed in

Holbein's painting, anticipates the contemporary freedom of the artist to create.

Rude when nude

Traditionally, the personification of this autonomous artistic spirit has been located in Italy, in the art of masters like Michelangelo Buonarroti and creations such as his statue of David preparing to fight Goliath (Fig. 1). For many, Michelangelo's *David* has become an iconic image of what the Renaissance is all about, the face (or body) that launched a thousand fridge magnets, and one of the most instantly recognizable art objects in the world.

Every year visitors crowd into Florence's Galleria dell'Accademia to look at Michelangelo's statue and be told that it is a timeless image of the perfection of the human form. Uniting classical antiquity with contemporary observation of anatomy, the statue captures David at a pregnant, contemplative moment prior to a dramatic scene of violence. Admiration for both the sculpture and its creator is heightened by the oft-quoted story that Michelangelo was commissioned to carve the statue in 1501 from a block of marble over five metres high which had been ruined by another sculptor nearly 40 years earlier.

The contemporary power of the statue has increased as *David* has been appropriated as a gay icon, a beautiful muscular naked boy about to get his man. The sensuously erotic nature of the sculpture also seems to confirm Michelangelo's stature as a great artist who also happened to be gay. This suggests that contemporary culture desires the Renaissance as a place where it can project its own hopes, fears, and preoccupations. If the

I.
Michelangelo's *David*: symbol of classical perfection or Renaissance rude boy?

Renaissance is supposed to be the origin of all civilized life, then one way of validating how we live our lives today is to find evidence of it in this period. However, this often blinds us to what actually motivated the creation of the art and culture of the Renaissance, and Michelangelo's *David* is no different in this respect.

The sculpture is in fact a highly coercive political object. The Republic of Florence commissioned the work as a symbol of political liberty triumphing over tyranny (many Florentines saw David's defeat over Goliath as an allegory of Florence's victory over similarly tyrannical foes such as Milan and the Medici family). A commission was drawn up in 1504 to decide where the completed statue should be publicly displayed to maximize its political impact. Michelangelo seized the sensitive commission as an opportunity to make a political and artistic name for himself. He also used the statue to confirm his status as a rather risqué artist. Previous sculptures of David had depicted the boy fully clothed. Michelangelo maximized the public impact of his towering sculpture by making his David naked, and justifying it through classical precedent (until recently some textbooks even placed a discrete fig-leaf over David's genitals). Michelangelo had little interest in the politics of the statue. By the time it was erected he had left Florence for more lucrative commissions in Rome. Later in his career he was similarly wooed by the Ottoman sultans to work on the architecture and decoration of the palaces and bazaars of Istanbul, another example of the opportunism that defined the activity of even the greatest Renaissance artists.

The wider Renaissance world

This brief consideration of Michelangelo is designed to acknowledge the cultural achievements of Italy, but this book revises the traditional focus on Italy as the exclusive origin of the Renaissance. Italy's undoubted importance has too often overshadowed the development of new ideas in northern Europe, the Iberian peninsula, the Islamic world, Southeast Asia, and Africa. In offering a more global perspective on the nature of the Renaissance, this book suggests that it would be more accurate to refer to a series of 'Renaissances' throughout these regions, each with their own highly specific and separate characteristics. These other Renaissances often overlapped and exchanged influences with the more classical and traditionally understood Renaissance centred on Italy. The Renaissance was also a remarkably international, fluid, and mobile phenomenon. Michelangelo's career captures something of this internationalism, with his links to Rome, Florence, and Istanbul. Holbein is an even better example of this cultural and geographical mobility. Born in Germany, he worked first in Basle, then in England as a court painter, and was heavily influenced by Italian art. The objects in his painting indicate that he absorbed cultural, political, and intellectual influences that were remarkably global. This made his painting strikingly hybrid, and very different from many of his Italian contemporaries. But this does not make him any less a Renaissance painter. If anything, his cultural mobility precisely defines his 'Renaissance' qualities.

Holbein's painting represents just some of the discoveries and achievements that took place during this period, which have now become synonymous with the term 'Renaissance'. These include oil painting, a relatively new technique that transformed the world of art; the invention of printing that revolutionized perceptions of knowledge and information; scientific invention and adaptation from the east, visible in the development of instruments such as the compass and the astrolabe, that transformed travel as well as ways of representing the world; new ways of doing business, often learnt from Arabic culture, such as paper money, deposit banking, and double entry bookkeeping that anticipated the dynamics of modern global capitalism; the development of geography that produced the first known terrestrial globe towards the end of the 15th century and which gave shape to so many of the complex transactions that took place across the globe; and the importing of new dyes and materials from the east, as in Dinteville's sumptuous clothes and the Turkish rug on the table, that transformed people's everyday domestic behaviour.

When was the Renaissance?

Today, there is a popular consensus that the term 'European Renaissance' refers to a profound and enduring upheaval and transformation in culture, politics, art, and society in Europe between the years 1400 and 1600. Different scholars offer alternative versions of this time span. Some focus on the importance of the 15th century, others see the quintessential manifestation of the Renaissance in the 16th century. However, in what follows it becomes clear that the disputes about dating the Renaissance have become so intense that the validity of the term is now in doubt. Does it have any meaning at all any more? Is it really possible to separate the Renaissance from the Middle Ages that preceded it, and the modern world that came after it? Does it have an objective identity or is it the projection of particular readings? Has it been invented to establish a convincing myth of European cultural superiority? To answer these questions, we need to understand how the term 'Renaissance' itself came into being.

No 16th-century audience would have recognized the term 'Renaissance'. The Italian word 'rinascita' ('rebirth') was often used in the 16th century to refer to the revival of classical culture.

But the specific French word 'Renaissance' was not used as a descriptive historical phrase until the middle of the 19th century. The first person to use the term was the French historian Jules Michelet, a French nationalist and republican deeply committed to the egalitarian principles of the French Revolution. Between 1833 and 1862 Michelet worked on his greatest project, the multi-volume *History of France*. He was vociferous in his condemnation of both the aristocracy and the church, and wrote the *History of the French Revolution* in support of the revolutionary ferment. With the ultimate failure of the 1848 revolution, Michelet fell into political disfavour. In 1855 he published his seventh volume of the *History*, entitled *La Renaissance*. For him the Renaissance meant:

> . . . the discovery of the world and the discovery of man. The sixteenth century . . . went from Columbus to Copernicus, from Copernicus to Galileo, from the discovery of the earth to that of the heavens. Man refound himself.

The scientific discoveries of explorers and thinkers like Columbus, Copernicus, and Galileo went hand in hand with the more philosophical understanding of what it meant to be an individual which Michelet identified in the writings of Rabelais, Montaigne, and Shakespeare. This new spirit was contrasted with what Michelet viewed as the 'bizarre and monstrous' quality of the Middle Ages. To him the Renaissance represented a progressive, democratic condition that celebrated the great virtues he valued—Reason, Truth, Art, and Beauty. According to Michelet, the Renaissance 'recognized itself as identical at heart with the modern age'.

Michelet was the first thinker to define the Renaissance as a decisive historical period in European culture that represented a crucial break with the Middle Ages, and which created a modern understanding of humanity and its place in the world. He also promoted the Renaissance as representing a certain spirit or attitude, as much as it referred to a specific historical period. Michelet's characterization of what the Renaissance represented sounds familiar to us today, but his understanding of when the Renaissance occurred is slightly less recognizable. Michelet's Renaissance does not happen in Italy in the 14th and 15th centuries, as we have come to expect. Instead, his Renaissance takes place in France in the 16th century. As a French nationalist, Michelet was eager to claim the Renaissance as a French phenomenon. As a republican he also rejected what he saw as 14th-century Italy's admiration for church and political tyranny as deeply undemocratic, and hence not part of the spirit of the Renaissance.

While Michelet's story of the Renaissance was and remains seductive, it was also affected as much by his own 19th-century circumstances as it was by the influence of the 16th century. In fact, the values of Michelet's Renaissance sound strikingly close to those of his cherished French Revolution: espousing the values of freedom, reason, and democracy, rejecting political and religious tyranny, and enshrining the spirit of freedom and the dignity of 'man'. Disappointed in the failure of the revolution of 1848, Michelet went back in time to find a moment where the values of liberty and egalitarianism triumphed and promised a modern world free of tyranny.

Swiss Renaissance

If Michelet invented the idea of the Renaissance, it was the Swiss academic Jacob Burckhardt who created the definitive portrait of the Renaissance as an Italian, predominantly 15th-century phenomenon. In 1860 Burckhardt published *The Civilisation of the Renaissance in Italy*. He argued that the peculiarities of political life in late 14th- and 15th-century Italy led to the creation of a recognizably modern individuality. The revival of classical antiquity, the discovery of the wider world, and the growing unease with organized religion, meant 'man became a spiritual *individual*'. Burckhardt deliberately contrasted this new development with the lack of individual awareness that for him defined the Middle Ages. Here, 'Man was conscious of himself only as a member of a race, people, party, family or corporation'. In other words, prior to the 15th century, people lacked a powerful sense of their individual identity. For Burckhardt, 15th-century Italy gave birth to 'Renaissance Man', what he called 'the first-born among the sons of modern Europe'. The result was what has become the now familiar account of the Renaissance: the birthplace of the modern world, created by Dante, Petrarch, Alberti, and Leonardo, characterized by the revival of classical culture, and over by the middle of the 16th century.

There are many flaws and omissions in Burckhardt's version of the Renaissance. Most noticeably, for a period celebrated for its visual art, Burckhardt says very little about Renaissance art or economic changes, and over-estimates what he sees as the sceptical, even 'pagan' approach to religion of the day. His focus is exclusively on Italy; he makes no attempt to see the Renaissance in relation to other cultures. His understanding of the terms 'individuality' and 'modern' also remain extremely vague. Like Michelet, Burckhardt's vision of the Renaissance reads like a version of his own personal circumstances. Burckhardt was an intellectual aristocrat, proud of his Protestant and republican Swiss individualism. While he hated the rise of 19th-century German imperial political power, he also feared the growth of industrial democracy and what he saw as its destruction of artistic beauty and taste. His subsequent vision of the Renaissance as a period where art and life were united, republicanism was celebrated but limited, and religion was tempered by the state, sounds like an idealized vision of his beloved Basle. Nevertheless, in arguing that the Renaissance is the foundation of modern life, Burckhardt's book has remained at the heart of Renaissance studies ever since; often criticized, but never completely dismissed.

Michelet and Burckhardt's celebrations of art and individuality as defining features of the Renaissance found their logical conclusion in England in Walter Pater's study *The Renaissance*, first published in 1873. Pater was an Oxford-educated don and aesthete, who used his study of the Renaissance as a vehicle for his belief in 'the love of art for its own sake'. Pater rejected the political, scientific, and economic aspects of the Renaissance as irrelevant, and saw 'a spirit of rebellion and revolt against the moral and religious ideas of the time' in the art of 15th-century painters like Botticelli, Leonardo, and Giorgione. This was not a democratic, political rebellion, but an aesthetic, hedonistic, even pagan celebration of what Pater called 'the pleasures of the senses and the imagination'. But what he called 'the spirit of the Renaissance' was not specific to the 15th century. He found traces of this 'love of the things of the intellect and the imagination for their own sake' as early as the 12th and as late as the 17th century. Many were scandalized by what they saw as Pater's decadent and irreligious book, but his views shaped the English-speaking world's view of the Renaissance for decades.

Michelet, Burckhardt, and Pater created a 19th-century idea of the Renaissance as more of a *spirit* than a historical period. The achievements of art and culture revealed a new attitude towards individuality and what it meant to be 'civilized'. The problem with this way of defining the Renaissance was that rather than offering an accurate historical account of what took place from the 15th century onwards it looked more like an ideal of 19th-century European society. These critics celebrated limited democracy, scepticism towards the church, the power of art and literature, and the triumph of European civilization over all others. These values underpinned 19th-century European imperialism. At a point in history that Europe was aggressively asserting its authority over most of the Americas, Africa, and Asia, people like Pater were creating a vision of the Renaissance that seemed to offer both an origin and a justification for European dominance over the rest of the globe.

Twentieth-century Renaissance

Twentieth-century understanding of the Renaissance in Europe and the United States remained very much in the shadow of Burckhardt. However, a more ambivalent view of the Renaissance increasingly defined these conceptions. One of the earliest challenges to Burckhardt, and to the idea of the Renaissance as a category in its own right, came in 1919, with the publication of Johan Huizinga's *The Waning of the Middle Ages*. Huizinga's book tried to address the ways in which northern European culture and society had been neglected in previous definitions of the Renaissance. It also challenged Burckhardt's period division between 'Middle Ages' and 'Renaissance'. Rather than seeing the

Middle Ages as the opposite of the Renaissance, Huizinga argued that the style and attitude that Burckhardt identified as 'Renaissance' was in fact the waning or declining spirit of the Middle Ages. Huizinga offered as an example the 15th-century Flemish art of Jan van Eyck:

> Both in form and in idea it is a product of the waning Middle Ages. If certain historians of art have discovered Renaissance elements in it, it is because they have confounded, very wrongly, realism and Renaissance. Now this scrupulous realism, this aspiration to render exactly all natural details, is the characteristic feature of the spirit of the expiring Middle Ages.

The detailed visual realism of van Eyck's *Arnolfini Double Portrait* (1434) (Fig. 18), or Holbein's *Ambassadors*, represents for Huizinga the end of a medieval tradition, not the birth of a Renaissance spirit of heightened artistic expression. While Huizinga did not reject the use of the term 'Renaissance', there remained little left of the idea that he did not see emanating from the Middle Ages. Huizinga's book offered a very pessimistic view of the ideal of the Renaissance celebrated by his 19th-century predecessors. Written in the midst of the First World War, it is hardly surprising that it could summon little enthusiasm for the idea of the Renaissance as the flowering of the superiority of European individuality and 'civilization'.

Huizinga's book did not demolish Burckhardt's vision of the Renaissance. Its focus on the literature and art of the 14th and 15th centuries strengthened an increasingly powerful tradition that placed intellectual possession of the Renaissance primarily in the hands of art historians. The most influential approach in this tradition was the iconological study of the Renaissance, developed by a German Jewish academic, Erwin Panofsky. Forced to leave Germany when the Nazis came to power in 1933, he took up a series of academic positions in New York. Panofsky agreed with Burckhardt that the revival of classical learning in Italy in the 15th century led to a 'respect for moral values' and 'learning and urbanity'. These were principles that Panofsky implied were worth fighting for in the face of the horrors of global warfare and the Holocaust that cast such a long shadow over the 20th century. As a result he formulated a more scientific approach to the art that held the key to the civilized values of the Renaissance, which he called 'Iconology'.

Panofsky argued that to understand any piece of Renaissance art it was necessary to understand its subject matter: images, stories, allegories. He termed this understanding *iconographical analysis*. He emphasized that this required a vast knowledge of the literary, philosophical, and political sources that went into the creation of the particular art object. Once this had been achieved, the critic could move towards 'Iconological interpretation'. This established the intrinsic, or symbolic, meaning of the work of art. Panofsky claimed that this scientific approach would 'reveal the basic attitude of a nation, a period, a class, a religious or philosophical persuasion—qualified by one personality and condensed into one work'. Iconology offered a science for understanding the essence, or 'attitude', of humanity, which could be revealed in art. Life could be most profoundly understood through art, with Renaissance art and its intense humanity forming the summit of this tradition. In his classic book *Studies in Iconology* (1939) Panofsky argued that Iconology is comparable to ethnology, which refers to 'a *science* of human races'. He concluded that the study and interpretation of art is a sign of how humane we are. For him, Renaissance art is the pinnacle of this humanity, as it marked the moment when mankind came to understand itself as humane and hence modern.

Panofsky illustrated his argument by comparing a 14th-century medieval image of a classical story with a late 15th-century picture of the same scene. Panofsky sees the medieval miniature showing Jove abducting Europa as lifeless and unable 'to visualize animal passions'. However, in Albrecht Dürer's drawing of the same scene (Fig. 2), completed around 1495, Panofsky finds 'the emotional vitality which was absent in the medieval representation'. It is a dynamic reworking of a classical story, vividly expressed and full of psychological intensity and emotion. Panofsky concludes that Dürer's drawing represents 'a humanistic but also a humane occurrence'. Here Renaissance

2.
Europe emerges:
Albrecht Dürer's
drawing 'The Rape
of Europa' (c.1495).

humanism as a way of thinking comes to define no less than what it means to be human.

Renaissance or early modern?

In the aftermath of the Second World War and the social and political upheavals of the 1960s, particularly the politicization of the humanities and the rise of feminism, the Renaissance was subjected to a profound reappraisal. One particularly influential response came from the United States. In 1980 the literary scholar Stephen Greenblatt published his book *Renaissance Self-Fashioning: From More to Shakespeare*. The book built on Burckhardt's view of the Renaissance as the point at which modern man was born. Drawing on new ways of thinking about sub-jectivity developed in psychoanalysis, anthropology, and social history, Greenblatt argued that the 16th century witnessed 'an increased self-consciousness about the fashioning of human identity'. Men (and on occasion women) learned to manipulate or 'fashion' their identities according to their circumstances. Like Burckhardt, Greenblatt saw this as the beginnings of a peculiarly modern phenomenon. As a critic of literature, Greenblatt saw Renaissance self-fashioning developing in the 16th century and continuing as late as the 17th century. For Greenblatt, the literature of the great writers of 16th-century England—Edmund Spenser, Christopher Marlowe, and William Shakespeare—produced fictional characters like Faustus and Hamlet that began to self-consciously reflect on and shape their own identities. In this respect they started to look and sound like modern men. The painting that Greenblatt used to intro-duce his theory of self-fashioning, and which adorned the cover of his book, was none other than Hans Holbein's *The Ambassadors*.

Greenblatt concluded that in the Renaissance 'the human subject itself began to seem remarkably unfree, the ideological product of the relations of power in a particular society'. Greenblatt's Renaissance was much more ambivalent than Burckhardt and Panofsky's versions. Writing as an American of Jewish descent, Greenblatt has subsequently explored both his admiration for the achievements of the Renaissance and his horror at its darker side, most specifically for him the rapacious colonization of the New World and the violent acts of anti-Semitism that took place throughout the 16th century.

Despite the title of Greenblatt's book, he, along with others, began to use the expression 'the early modern period' to define the Renaissance. The term came from social history and proposed a more sceptical relationship between the Renaissance and the modern world than the vague and idealistic accounts of Michelet and Burckhardt. It also turned the idea of the Renaissance into a period of history, rather than the cultural 'spirit' proposed by 19th-century writers. The term 'early modern' still suggested that what took place between 1400 and 1600 deeply influenced and affected the modern world. It also retained a politically progressive belief that an understanding of the past can help to understand and transform the present. Instead of focusing on how the Renaissance itself looked back to the classical world, 'early modern' suggests that the period involved a forward-looking attitude that prefigured our own modern world.

The concept of the early modern period also enabled an exploration of topics and subjects not previously thought fit for consideration in relation to the Renaissance. Scholars like

Greenblatt and Natalie Zemon Davis in her book *Society and Culture in Early Modern France* (1975) explored the social roles of peasants, artisans, transvestites, and 'unruly' women. Most significant was the analysis of the role of women in the history of the Renaissance, heavily influenced by the publication in 1977 of Joan Kelly-Gadol's article 'Did Women Have a Renaissance?'. Critics began to realize that categories like 'Jew', 'Muslim', 'Black', or even 'Woman' changed through time and across history. Identity was not fixed and unchangeable, as Burckhardt had implied in his celebration of 'modern' man: it was fluid and contingent. This allowed writers to understand that if identity had been different in the past, then it could also change in the future.

1492: looking east and west

1992 marked the quincentenary of Columbus' first landfall in America, and led to a spate of conferences, exhibitions, and books reflecting on the complex legacy of the Genoese navigator's voyage. However, rather than turning into a celebration of Columbus' achievements, the anniversary became the occasion for a radical reassessment of the role of the Renaissance in global history. The National Gallery of Art in Washington organized an international exhibition entitled 'Circa 1492: Art in the Age of Exploration', which viewed Columbus' voyages in the context of wider events in 15th-century Europe, Africa, Asia, and the Far East. Drawing on more sceptical approaches to the Renaissance, the exhibition and accompanying catalogue examined the intellectual and scientific achievements of the period alongside its more baleful consequences: colonization, slavery, religious conflict, and the rise of European imperialism.

The anniversary of Columbus' first voyage led a new generation of scholars to think about how Europe's discovery of the New World to the west was based upon an understanding of the Old World to the east. 1492 was also the year that Columbus' royal patrons, Ferdinand and Isabella, expelled both the Jewish and Arabic communities from Spain. In the account of his first voyage, dedicated to Ferdinand and Isabella, Columbus wrote: 'having expelled all the Jews from your domains in that same month of January, your Highnesses commanded me to go with an adequate fleet to these parts of India [the Americas] ... I departed from the city of Granada on Saturday 12 May and went to the port of Palos, where I prepared three ships.' Columbus understood his voyage to the New World as a mission to conquer and convert the people he found there, in the same way that Ferdinand and Isabella aimed to conquer the Jewish and Muslim communities of Spain. This was a much more sinister version of the voyages of discovery than the one provided by Michelet and Burckhardt. It also showed that, until the end of the 15th century, Christians, Muslims, and Jews had amicably exchanged ideas and objects, despite their religious differences.

Today scholars are beginning to realize that, despite Ferdinand and Isabella's attempt to eradicate the Renaissance bazaars of Spain at the end of the 15th century, the spirit of mutual exchange between east and west continued throughout the 16th century. These connections were responsible for some of the greatest creations of what we today call the European Renaissance. While the discovery of America to the west profoundly transformed how Europeans understood their place in an expanding world, the ongoing encounters with the east were also crucial to how Europe began to define itself regionally, both politically and creatively.

1. A GLOBAL RENAISSANCE

Whose Renaissance is it anyway?

One of the problems with the classic definitions of the Renaissance is that they celebrate the achievements of European civilization to the exclusion of all others. It is no coincidence that the period that witnessed the invention of the term was also the moment at which Europe was most aggressively asserting its imperial dominance across the globe. The Renaissance Man invented by Michelet and Burckhardt was white, male, cultured, and convinced of his cultural superiority. In this respect, Renaissance Man sounds like the Victorian ideal of an imperial adventurer or colonial official. Rather than describing the world of the 15th and 16th centuries, these writers were in fact describing their own world. This chapter rejects this approach and focuses on the cultural and commercial exchanges between an amorphous Europe and the societies to its east. It argues that Renaissance Europe defined and measured itself in relation to the wealth and splendour of the east, a fact that has been overlooked due to the influence of the 19th-century version of the Renaissance until recently.

An image used by Panofsky to define what he saw as the shift from the attitude of the Middle Ages to the spirit of the Renaissance offers a good place to start. The image is Dürer's drawing 'The Rape of Europa' (Fig. 2). Panofsky sees this image as part of a broader change in emotional and intellectual perceptions of individuality and the wider world. It is an image full of emotion, action, and life. It defines the humanist spirit of the Renaissance, the spirit that, according to Panofsky, is the basis of humanity itself. Crucially it is also an image of the birth of Europe. In classical mythology Europa was the daughter of the King of Tyre in Asia. The amorous Jupiter (disguised as a bull) abducted Europa from the seashore and carried her off from Asia to Crete. This has served mythically as a metaphor for the birth of the continent of Europe. As well as capturing a new spirit of 'the world and of man', Dürer's drawing also encapsulates the moment when Europe as we now know it started to define itself as such. The concept of 'Europe' is born in the Renaissance. According to Panofsky, so is modern humanity. The implication is that cultures existing before this moment and beyond the boundaries of Europe are excluded from this tradition of 'humaneness'. Panofsky's reading of the drawing is entirely positive: he seems impervious to the negative associations involved in the creation of 'Europe', and the fact that this act of creation is based on an act of violation. It also establishes the notion that the separation of Asia and Europe was the basis for the creation of Europe and its Renaissance—that is, that Europe could only be defined against the east, in opposition to it. But looking back at the Renaissance today, we can see that this approach is inaccurate. It excludes the peoples and cultures whose presence was central to creating the spirit of the Renaissance, a Renaissance more diverse and less unified than has often been assumed.

Contrast this drawing with a more elaborate painting that had been commissioned just three years before Dürer's arrival in Venice: Gentile and Giovanni Bellini's painting *Saint Mark Preaching in Alexandria* (Fig. 3). Grand in scale, painstakingly executed over several years, it was commissioned in 1492 by the

3.
Gentile and
Giovanni Bellini's
*Saint Mark
Preaching in
Alexandria*
(1504–7) captures
Europe's
fascination with
the culture,
architecture, and
communities of
the east.

Scuola di San Marco, a powerful Venetian fraternity, to decorate their new residence (which still stands to this day). It was finally completed in 1507.

The Bellini painting depicts St Mark, the founder of the Christian Church in Alexandria, where he was martyred around AD 75, and subsequently the patron saint of Venice. In the painting Mark stands in a pulpit, preaching to a group of oriental women swathed in white mantles. Behind Mark stand a group of Venetian noblemen, while in front of the saint is an extraordinary array of Oriental figures that mingle easily with more Europeans. They include Egyptian Mamluks, North African 'Moors', Turks, Persians, Ethiopians, and Tartars. The drama of the action takes place in the bottom third of the painting; the rest of the canvas is dominated by the dramatic landscape of Alexandria. A sumptuous domed Byzantine basilica, an imaginative recreation of St Mark's Alexandrian church, dominates the backdrop. In the piazza Oriental figures converse, some on horseback, others leading camels and a giraffe. The houses that face onto the square are adorned with Egyptian grilles and tiles. Islamic carpets and rugs hang from the windows. The minarets, columns, and pillars that make up the skyline are a mixture of recognizable Alexandrian landmarks and the Bellinis' own invention. The basilica itself is an eclectic mixture of elements of the Church of San Marco in Venice and Hagia Sophia in Constantinople, while the towers and columns in the distance correspond to some of Alexandria's most famous landmarks, many of which had already been emulated in the architecture of Venice itself.

At first the painting appears to be a pious image of the Christian martyr preaching to a group of 'unbelievers'. However, this only tells one side of the story. Although Mark is dressed as an ancient Roman, in keeping with his life in 1st-century Alexandria, the garments of the audience are recognizably late 15th century, as are the surrounding buildings. The Bellinis are at pains to depict the intermingling of communities and cultures in a scene that evokes both the western church and the eastern bazaar. The painting is an ingenious combination of two worlds: the contemporary and the classical. At the same time as evoking the world of 1st-century Alexandria and the life of St Mark, the artists are also keen to portray Venice's relationship with contemporary, late 15th-century Alexandria. Commissioned to paint a story of the history of Venice's patron saint, they cleverly depict St Mark in a contemporary setting that would have been recognizable to many wealthy and influential Venetians. This is a familiar feature of Renaissance art and literature, and something that unites the painting with Dürer's sketch of Europa: dressing the contemporary world up in the clothes of the past as a way of understanding the present.

West meets east

Dürer and the Bellinis were fascinated by both the myths and the reality of the world to the east of what is today seen as Renaissance Europe. Dürer's celebration of a violent energy behind Europe's creation is also an image of east–west interaction that suggests that the late 15th century was aware of how Europe looked to the east to define itself artistically and culturally. The Bellinis are concerned with the more specific nature of this eastern world, and in particular the customs, architecture, and culture of Arabic Alexandria, one of Venice's long-standing trading partners. Dürer and the Bellinis did not dismiss the Mamluks of Egypt, the Ottomans of Turkey, or the Persians of Central Asia as ignorant or barbaric. Instead, they were acutely aware that these cultures possessed many things that the city states of Europe desired. These included precious commodities, technical, scientific, and artistic knowledge, and ways of doing business that came from the bazaars of the east, and which were way beyond anything understood in what we today would call the west. The Bellini painting of St Mark preaching in Alexandria reflects how Europe began to define itself not in opposition to the mysterious east, but through an extensive and complex exchange of ideas and materials.

The Bellinis' Venetian contemporaries were explicit about their reliance upon such transactions with the east. In 1493 the Venetian diarist Mario Sanudo noted:

> The Venetians, just as they were merchants in the beginning, continue to trade every year; they send galleys to Flanders, the Barbary Coast, Beirut, Alexandria, the Greek lands and Aigues-Mortes.

Sanudo appreciated that Venice was perfectly situated as a

commercial intermediary, able to receive commodities from these eastern bazaars, and then transport them to the markets of northern Europe. Writing at the same time as the Bellinis worked on their painting of St Mark, Canon Pietro Casola reported with amazement the impact that this flow of goods from the east had upon Venice itself:

> Something may be said about the quality of merchandise in the said city, although not nearly the whole truth, because it is inestimable. Indeed it seems as if all the world flocks here, and that human beings have concentrated there all their force for trading . . . who could count the many shops so well furnished that they almost seem warehouses, with so many cloths of every make—tapestry, brocades and hangings of every design, carpets of every sort, camlets [sheets] of every colour and texture, silks of every kind; and so many warehouses full of spices, groceries and drugs, and so much beautiful wax! These things stupefy the beholder.

East–west trade in these goods had been taking place throughout the Mediterranean for centuries, but its volume increased following the end of the Crusades, when the easy flow of goods between Arab and Christian communities was re-established. From the 14th century Venice fought competitors like Genoa and Florence to establish its dominance of the trade from the Red Sea and the Indian Ocean that terminated at Alexandria. Venetian and Genoese trading centres and consuls were established in Alexandria, Damascus, Aleppo, and even further afield. Europe exported textiles, especially woollens, glassware, soap, paper, copper, salt, dried fruits, and, more than anything, silver and gold. Commodities imported from the east ranged from spices (black pepper, nutmeg, cloves, and cinnamon), cotton, silk, satin, velvet, and carpets to opium, tulips, sandalwood, porcelain, horses, rhubarb, and precious stones, as well as vivid dyes and pigments used in textile manufacture and painting.

While Europe predominantly exported bulk goods such as timber, wool, and semi-precious metals, it tended to import luxury and high-value goods, whose impact upon the culture and consumption of communities from Venice to London was gradual but profound. Every sphere of life was affected, from eating to painting. 15th-century cookbooks include recipes for rabbit using ground almonds, saffron, ginger, cypress root, cinnamon, sugar, cloves, and nutmeg. For a banquet of forty guests one household account book lists the following quantities of spices required: 'one pound of colombine powder ... half a pound of ground cinnamon ... two pounds of sugar ... one ounce of saffron ... a quarter pound of cloves and grains of guinea pepper (grains of paradise) ... an eighth of a pound of pepper ... an eighth of a pound of galingale ... an eighth of a pound of nutmeg'. Used as drugs, medicines, perfume and even adopted for religious ceremonies, such rare commodities may have been small in quantity, but were widespread in their impact upon every sphere of life. As the domestic economy changed with this influx of exotic goods, so did art and culture. The palette of painters like the Bellinis was also expanded by the addition of pigments like lapis lazuli, vermilion, and cinnabar, all of which were imported from the east via Venice, and provided Renaissance paintings with their characteristic brilliant blues and reds. The loving detail with which the Bellini painting of St Mark reproduces silk, velvet, muslin, cotton, tiling, carpets, even livestock, reflected the Bellinis' awareness of how these exchanges with the bazaars of the east were transforming the sights, smells, and tastes of the world, and the ability of the artist to reproduce them.

The eastern bazaars of Cairo, Aleppo, and Damascus were also responsible for literally shaping the architecture of Venice itself. The Venetian art historian Giuseppe Fiocco once described Venice as a 'colossal *suq*', and more recently architectural historians have noticed how many characteristics of the city were based on direct emulation of eastern design and decor. The Rialto market, with its linear buildings arranged in parallel to the main arteries is strikingly similar to the layout of the Syrian trading capital of Aleppo, while the windows, arches, and decorative façades of the Doge's Palace and the Palazzo Ducale all draw their inspiration from the mosques, bazaars, and palaces of eastern cities like Cairo, Acre, and Tabriz, where Venetian merchants had traded for centuries. Venice was a quintessential Renaissance city, not just for its combination of commerce and aesthetic luxury, but also for its admiration and emulation of eastern cultures.

Credits and debits

Economic and political historians have fiercely debated the reasons for the changes in demand and consumption within this period. The belief in the flowering of the social and cultural spirit of the Renaissance is also strangely at odds with the general belief that the 14th and 15th centuries experienced a profound period of economic depression. Prices fell and wages slumped. The problem was made worse by the devastating impact of the outbreak of Black Death in 1348. However, one of the consequences of widespread disease and death, just like warfare, is often radical social change and upheaval. Such was the case in Europe in the aftermath of the plague. As well as disease, warfare ravaged the region. The Flemish civil wars (1293–1328), the

Muslim–Christian conflict in Spain and North Africa (1291–1341), the Genoese–Venetian wars (1291–9; 1350–5; 1378–81), and the Hundred Years War across northern Europe (1336–1453) all disrupted trade and agriculture, creating a cyclical pattern of inflation and sudden deflation. One consequence of all this death, disease, and warfare was a concentration on urban life, and an accumulation of wealth in the hands of a small but rich elite, whose conspicuous consumption began to define the cultured extravagance that we call the Renaissance. This was the lavish display of luxury and ornamentation that Johan Huizinga saw in his study of the Burgundian courts of northern Europe and which Jacob Burckhardt identified in 15th-century Italy.

As in most periods of history, where some people experience depression and decline, others see opportunity and fortune. Venice in particular took advantage of the situation to capitalize on the growing demand for luxury goods, and developed new ways of moving larger quantities of merchandise between east and west. Their older 'galleys', narrow oared ships, were gradually replaced by the heavy, round-bottomed masted ships, or 'cogs', used to transport bulky goods such as timber, grain, salt, fish, and iron between northern European ports. These cogs were able to transport over 300 'barrels' of merchandise (one 'barrel' equalled 900 litres), more than three times the amount possible aboard the older galley. By the end of the 15th century the three-masted 'caravel' was developed. Based on Arabic designs, it took up to 400 barrels of merchandise and was also considerably faster than the cog.

As the amount and speed of distribution of merchandise increased, so ways of transacting business also changed. Lying on his deathbed in 1423, the Venetian Doge Tomaso Mocenigo drew up a rhetorical balance sheet of the commercial state of his city, which gives some idea of the growing scale and complexity of trade and finance in the period:

> The Florentines bring to Venice yearly 16,000 bales of the finest cloth which is sold in Naples, Sicily and the East. They export wool, silk, gold, silver, raisins and sugar to the value of 392,000 ducats in Lombardy. Milan spends annually, in Venice, 90,000 ducats; Monza, 56,000; Commo, Tortona, Novara, Cremona, 104,000 ducats each . . . and in their turn they import into Venice cloth to the value of 900,000 ducats, so that there is a total turnover of 2,800,000 ducats. Venetian exports to the whole world represent annually ten million ducats; her imports amount to another ten million. On these twenty millions she made a profit of four million, or interest at the rate of twenty per cent.

The financial reality was probably messier than Mocenigo's neat sums suggest. Nevertheless, the complexity of balancing the import and export of both essential and luxury international goods and calculating credit, profit, and rates of interest sounds so familiar to us today that it is easy to see why the Renaissance is often referred to as the birthplace of modern capitalism. But it would be inaccurate to say that this was an exclusively European development. Just as European merchants trafficked in the exotic goods of the east, so they incorporated Arabic and Islamic ways of doing business through their exposure to the bazaars and trading centres throughout North Africa, the Middle East, and Persia.

At the very beginning of the 13th century the Pisan merchant Leonardo Pisan, known as Fibonacci, was using his commercial exposure to Arabic ways of reckoning profit and loss to write a series of highly influential books on mathematics. In 1202 he completed his study of mathematics and calculation entitled *Liber abbaci*. The beginning of the book reveals something of

Fibonacci's life and his debt to Arabic learning in the field of mathematics:

> I joined my father after his assignment by his homeland Pisa as an officer in the customhouse located in Bugia [in Algeria] for the Pisan merchants who thronged to it. He had me marvellously instructed in the Arabic–Hindu numerals and calculation. I enjoyed so much the instruction that I later continued to study mathematics while on business trips to Egypt, Syria, Greece, Sicily, and Provence and there enjoyed discussions and disputations with the scholars of those places. Returning to Pisa I composed this book of fifteen chapters which comprises what I feel is best of the Hindu, Arabic, and Greek Methods.

In his commercial exchanges with Arab merchants in the eastern bazaars, Fibonacci realized that the European practice of using roman numerals and the abacus was awkward and time-consuming. Hindu–Arabic numerals were vastly superior and allowed for complex and increasingly abstract solutions to the calculation of profit and loss. As a result Fibonacci carefully explained the nature of the Hindu–Arabic numerals from 'o' to '9', the use of the decimal point, and their application to practical commercial problems involving addition, subtraction, multiplication, division, and the gauging of weights and measures, as well as bartering, charging of interest, and exchanging currency. While this may seem straightforward today, it is worth remembering that signs for addition (+), subtraction (−), and multiplication (×) were unknown in Europe before Fibonacci.

The kind of Arabic commercial practice that Fibonnaci borrowed from was itself drawn from much earlier Arabic developments in mathematics and geometry. For instance, the basic principles of algebra were adopted from the Arabic term for restoration, 'al-jabru'. Around AD 825 the Persian astronomer Abu Ja'far Mohammed ibn Mûsâ al-Khowârizmî wrote a book which included the rules of arithmetic for the decimal positional number system, called *Kitāb al-jābr w'al-muqābala* ('Rules of restoration and reduction'). His Latinized name provided the basis for the further study of one of the cornerstones of modern mathematics: the algorithm.

The woodcut illustrating Bernhard von Breydenbach's *Peregrinationes*, first published in 1486 (Fig. 4), is a concise depiction of how trade, mathematics, and amicable exchanges with Arabic culture all went hand in hand throughout the 14th and 15th centuries. This is the first known European instance of the reproduction of Arabic writing in a printed book. The illustration shows a version of the Arabic alphabet, with an image of a moneychanger transacting business directly beneath. It encompasses the cultural, linguistic, and financial exchanges that travellers and traders like Breydenbach would have come to expect from any time spent in the bazaars of the east. The point was emphasized by Gaspar Nicolas, author of an arithmetic book published in Portuguese in 1519, who pointed out, 'I am printing this arithmetic because it is a thing so necessary in Portugal for transactions with the merchants of India, Persia, Arabia, Ethiopia, and other places.'

Fibonacci's new methods were gradually adopted in the trading centres of Venice, Florence, and Genoa, as they realized that new ways of keeping track of increasingly complex and international commercial transactions were needed. Payment on goods was often provided in silver or gold bullion, but as sales increased and more than two people became involved in any one business deal, new ways of trading were required. One of the

4.
Bernhard von Breydenbach's woodcut of the Arabic alphabet and moneychanger (1486) shows how closely Europe observed the customs, language, and commerce of the east.

most significant innovations was the bill of exchange, the earliest example of paper money. A bill of exchange was the ancestor of the modern cheque, which originated from the medieval Arabic term 'sakk'. When you write a cheque, you are drawing on your creditworthiness at a bank. Your bank will honour the cheque when the holder presents it for payment. A 14th-century trader would similarly pay for a consignment of merchandise with a paper bill of exchange drawn from a powerful merchant family, who would honour the bill when it was presented either on a specific later date, or upon delivery of the goods. Merchant families that guaranteed such transactions on pieces of paper soon transformed themselves into bankers as well as merchants. The merchant turned banker made money on these transactions by charging interest based on the amount of time it took for the bill to be repaid and through manipulating the rate of exchange between different international currencies.

God's bankers

The medieval church still forbade usury, defined as the charging of interest on a loan. The theologian St Thomas Aquinas argued that 'to receive usury for money lent is in itself unjust since it is the sale of what does not exist; whereby, inequality results, which is contrary to justice'. The religious tenets of both Christianity and Islam officially forbade the charging of interest on loans. In practice, both cultures found loopholes to maximize financial profit. Merchant bankers could disguise the charging of interest by nominally lending money in one currency and then collecting it in a different currency. Built into this process was a favourable rate of exchange that allowed the merchant banker to profit by a percentage of the original amount. The banker therefore held money on 'deposit' for merchants and in return established sufficient 'credit' for other merchants to accept their bills of exchange as a form of money in its own right. Another solution was to employ Jewish merchants to handle credit transactions and act as commercial mediators between the two religions, for the simple reason that Jews were free of any official religious prohibition against usury. From this historical accident emerged the anti-Semitic stereotype of Jews and their supposed connection with international finance, a direct product of Christian and Muslim hypocrisy. This hypocrisy is dramatically captured in both Marlowe's play *The Jew of Malta* (*c*.1590) and Shakespeare's *The Merchant of Venice* (1594), in their depictions of Jewish merchants who are ultimately portrayed as less rapacious and selfish than the Christian and Islamic communities within which they live.

The accumulating wealth and status of merchant bankers laid the foundations for the political power and artistic innovation that today characterizes the European Renaissance. The famous Medici family who dominated Florentine politics and culture throughout the 15th century started out life as merchant bankers. In 1397 Giovanni di Bicci de' Medici established the Medici Bank in Florence, which soon perfected the art of double-entry bookkeeping and accounting, deposit and transfer banking, maritime insurance, and the profitable circulation of bills of exchange. The Medici Bank also became 'God's banker' by transferring the papacy's funds throughout Europe. By 1429 the humanist scholar and Florentine chancellor Poggio Bracciolini could venture the opinion that 'money is necessary as the sinews that maintain the state', and that it was 'very advantageous, both for the common welfare and for civic life'. Examining the impact of trade and commerce on cities, he could rightly ask, 'how many magnificent houses, distinguished villas, churches, colonnades, and hospitals have been constructed in our own time' with the money generated by the great merchant houses of the likes of the Medici in Florence? Figures like Fibonacci and Bracciolini understood that it was trade and exchange with the east, and the adoption of more systematic ways of doing business that created the conditions for Renaissance art, culture, and consumption. Speculation, exchange, risk, and profit are all terms taken from trade and commerce. However, by the end of the 15th century such terms had also become central to people's understanding of the world and their own personal identity.

The grand Turks

In 1453, the Hundred Years War between England and France came to an end. One consequence of the peace was an intensification of trade between northern and southern Europe. At the other end of Europe 1453 witnessed another equally momentous event. This was the year that the Islamic Ottoman Empire finally conquered the seat of the thousand-year-old Byzantine Empire, Constantinople. The fall of Constantinople to the Turkish Ottoman forces signalled a decisive shift in international political power and confirmed the Ottomans as the most powerful empire that Europe had seen since the days of the Roman Empire.

The Ottoman Empire emerged in the 13th century from a small Turkish tribe based in Anatolia in western Turkey whose military conquests increasingly encroached on the territories of the crumbling Byzantine Empire to the west. The first Christian

Roman Emperor, Constantine, renamed Byzantium Constantinople in 330. By 1054 the differences between the western Catholic Church and the Eastern Orthodox Church based in Constantinople were so irreconcilable that the two churches refused to acknowledge the authority of the other, an event known as the Great Schism. As the Turks closed in on the prize of Constantinople throughout the 1430s, increasingly desperate attempts to unify the western and eastern churches and defend the city collapsed. In the spring of 1453 over 100,000 Turkish troops laid siege to Constantinople, and on 28 May the Sultan Mehmed II, afterwards referred to as 'Mehmed the Conqueror', finally captured the city. Traditionally the fall of Constantinople has been seen as a catastrophe for Christianity and many contemporary church leaders were horrified by the news. The renowned humanist scholar Aeneas Silvius Piccolomini (later Pope Pius II) wrote to Pope Nicholas V:

> But what is that terrible news recently reported about Constantinople? ... Who can doubt that the Turks will vent their wrath upon the churches of God? I grieve that the world's most famous temple, Hagia Sophia, will be destroyed or defiled. I grieve that countless basilicas of the saints, marvels of architecture, will fall in ruins or be subjected to the defilements of Mohammed. What can I say about the books without number there which are not yet known in Italy? Alas, how many names of great men will now perish? This will be a second death to Homer and a second destruction of Plato.

As the capital of the Byzantine Empire, Constantinople was one of the last connections between the world of classical Rome and 15th-century Italy. It acted as a conduit for the recovery of much of the learning of classical culture. Piccolomini saw the city's fall as a repeat of the fall of the Roman Empire itself, its culture, learning, and architecture destroyed by the 'barbarian' hordes. The only difference was that this time they were Muslims.

In fact Mehmed was not the barbaric despot often evoked in the western historical imagination. His affinity with the political ambitions and cultural tastes of his Italian counterparts was stronger than is often imagined. While directing the siege of Constantinople, Mehmed employed several Italian humanists who 'read to the Sultan daily from ancient historians such as Laertius, Herodotus, Livy and Quintus Curtius and from chronicles of the popes and the Lombard kings'. Mehmed and his predecessors had spent decades conquering much of the territory of the classical Graeco-Roman world to which 15th-century Italian humanism looked for much of its inspiration. It is therefore hardly surprising that the cultured Mehmed should share similar cultural and historical influences and aspirations, and that his imperial achievements were 'in no way inferior to those of Alexander the Macedonian' (Alexander the Great), as one of Mehmed's Greek chroniclers told him. Another admiring scholar, George of Trebizond, wrote to Mehmed telling him, 'no one doubts that you are emperor of the Romans. Whoever holds by right the centre of the empire is emperor and the centre of the empire is Constantinople'. Mehmed appeared surprised at Italy's anxiety regarding his conquest of Greece. Claiming that the Turks and Italians shared a common Trojan heritage, he presumed that the Italians would be pleased at his victory over a mutual old enemy! Despite Piccolomini's fears of the destruction and religious desecration of Constantinople, Mehmed immediately embarked upon an ambitious building programme to support his claims to imperial authority. This involved repopulating the city with Jewish and Christian merchants and craftsmen, founding the Great Bazaar that established the city's pre-eminence as an international trading centre, and renaming it Istanbul, meaning 'throne' or 'capital'.

Many European powers saw Mehmed's rise to power as an opportunity rather than a catastrophe. Within months of the fall of Constantinople both Venice and Genoa sent envoys to success-fully renew trading relations with the city and the vastly enlarged Ottoman territories. By spring 1454 Venice had signed a peace treaty with Mehmed allowing it preferable commercial privileges. The Venetian Doge insisted 'it is our intention to live in peace and friendship with the Turkish emperor'. The resumption of amicable commercial relations was also matched by cultural and artistic transactions. In 1461 Sigismondo Malatesta, the feared Lord of Rimini, sent his court artist Matteo de' Pasti to Istanbul 'to paint and sculpt' the sultan, in the hope of formal-izing a military alliance with the Ottomans against Venice. The Italian architects Filarete and Michelozzo were also both wooed by Mehmed as possible designers for his ambitious new palace, the Topkapi Saray, which, according to one 16th-century Venetian ambassador, 'everyone acknowledges to be the most beautiful, the most convenient, and most miraculous in the world'.

Rather than destroying the classical texts of the ancient world, Mehmed's library, much of which still remains in the Topkapi Saray in Istanbul, reveals that he coveted such books as zealously as his Italian counterparts. Mehmed's library included copies of Ptolemy's *Geography*, Avicenna's *Canones*, Aquinas's *Summa contra Gentiles*, Homer's *Iliad*, and other texts in Greek, Hebrew, and Arabic. So great was Mehmed's reputation that in 1482 the Florentine humanist Francesco Berlinghieri dedicated his new Latin translation of Ptolemy's *Geography* to 'Mehmed of the Ottomans, illustrious prince and lord of the throne of God'. When Berlinghieri heard that the sultan had died suddenly, he quickly corrected his translation and dedicated it to Mehmed's successor, Bayezid II! In 1479 the Doge of Venice 'loaned' Gentile Bellini to Mehmed. Giorgio Vasari writes, 'Gentile had been there [in Constantinople] no long time when he portrayed the Emperor Mehmed from the life so well, that it was held a miracle'. This is the beautiful portrait that Bellini painted of Mehmed (Plate 2) that still hangs in the National Gallery in London. Bellini returned to Venice laden with gifts from Mehmed, and 'in addition to many privileges, there was placed around his neck a chain wrought in the Turkish manner, equal in weight to 250 gold crowns'. This gift throws new light on the painting *Saint Mark Preaching in Alexandria*, by Gentile and his brother Giovanni. At the foot of Mark's pulpit, positioned in the foreground, is an unmistakable self-portrait of Gentile; round his neck hangs the chain presented to him by Mehmed. Here is Bellini proudly displaying the fruits of Mehmed's patronage, and using his experiences in Istanbul to add exotic detail to his depiction of Alexandria. Mehmed's patronage is evidently not a source of embarrassment, but a mark of distinction.

Several Italian rulers acknowledged Mehmed's power by commissioning their own art objects in his honour. In April 1478 Giuliano de' Medici, brother of Lorenzo de' Medici, was murdered by Bernardo Bandini Baroncello in the infamous 'Pazzi Conspiracy'. Bernardo fled to Istanbul, but was arrested on Mehmed's orders and returned to Florence where he was subsequently executed for murder. To express his gratitude Lorenzo commissioned the Florentine artist Bertoldo di Giovanni to make a portrait medal of Mehmed. The front of the medal shows

Mehmed's profile, while the back depicts Mehmed in triumph, riding a chariot that contains personifications of the vanquished territories in Europe and Asia now under his control. Like other portrait medals made for Mehmed, this medal draws on classical Graeco-Roman themes and motifs that Lorenzo de' Medici obviously believed would be recognizable to Mehmed. This was a flattering art commission, designed to celebrate the achievements of a rival, but one who shared a common artistic and intellectual heritage.

There were no clear geographical or political barriers between east and west in the 15th century. It is a much later, 19th-century belief in the absolute cultural and political separation of the Islamic east and Christian west that has obscured the easy exchange of trade, art, and ideas between these two cultures. Europe was very aware that the culture, customs, and religion of Islam were very different from its own, and the two sides were often in direct military conflict with each other. However, the point is that material and commercial exchanges between them were largely unaffected by political hostility: instead the competitiveness of business transactions and cultural exchanges produced a fertile environment for development on both sides.

East–west conflict persisted, but Mehmed's imperial successors kept up the cultural, political, and commercial dialogue with Europe, exchanging everything from silk, horses, rugs, and tapestries to porcelain, tulips, and armaments. In 1482 Mehmed's son Prince Cem Sultan unsuccessfully challenged his brother, the future Bayezid II, for the vacant imperial crown. He fled to Rhodes, then France, and was finally held in Rome from 1489 under papal supervision. His mysterious death in Naples in 1495 ended European hopes of placing a sympathetic figure on the

Ottoman throne. However, this did not prevent Bayezid from continuing to woo Italian merchants and artists, inviting both Leonardo and Michelangelo to work on commissions in Istanbul. The accession of Sultan Süleyman the Magnificent in 1520 intensified artistic and diplomatic exchanges. Süleyman established a lively two-way trade in horses, tapestries, and jewellery. Pietro Aretino, one of Italy's most renowned humanist scholars, was particularly impressed by Süleyman, and wrote to offer his scholarly services in 1532. In 1533 the Dermoyen tapestry firm dispatched a team of weavers and merchants to Istanbul to design tapestries for the sultan. The firm was clearly impressed by Süleyman's investment in lavish imperial art objects, such as the dazzling imperial crown he bought from a consortium of Venetian goldsmiths in 1532. The Turks were again laying siege to Vienna at the time, and Süleyman would ride around the city walls wearing his magnificent crown, a deliberate provocation to the city's Hapsburg defenders. Such behaviour delighted the French, Süleyman's long-standing allies. By the 1570s the Ottomans were also allied to the English crown, which sought Turkish support in its opposition to the imperial ambitions of the Spanish King Philip II. The Turks became such powerful political brokers in late 16th-century Europe that the French humanist Michel de Montaigne concluded that 'the mightiest, yea the best settled estate that is now in the world is that of the Turkes'.

The winds of change

Rather than shutting off cultural contact between east and west, once it was in control of Constantinople the Ottoman Empire simply charged for such exchanges. Overland trade routes into

Persia, Central Asia, and China were heavily taxed by the Ottoman administration, but this just created new ways of doing
business. The end of the Hundred Years War stimulated a greater
circulation of trade between northern and southern Europe,
intensifying the demand for exotic goods from the east. This
accelerated the pace and scale of commercial exchange and led
Christian European states to seek ways of circumventing the
heavy tariffs placed on their transportation of goods from east to
west. Most eastern merchandise was paid for in European gold
and silver bullion. As the ore mines in Central Europe began to
run dry and tariffs escalated, new sources of revenue were
needed: this led directly to an increase in exploration and
discovery.

For centuries gold had trickled into Europe via North Africa
and the trans-Saharan caravan routes. The Jewish mapmaker
Abraham Cresques encapsulated the European desire for African
gold in his *Catalan Atlas*, made in 1375 for Charles V of France
(Plate 3). In the panel representing north-west Africa, Cresques
depicts the fabled 'Musa Mansu', lord of Guinea, seated above
two of the key places involved in the Saharan movement of gold—
Mali and Timbuktu. In his hands he holds a gold orb, and the
legend to his right reads, 'So abundant is the gold which is found
in his country that he is the richest and most noble king in the
land'.

Exotic as Cresques' map looks, it offers a reasonably accurate
understanding of the movement of gold from the mines of Sudan
to the commercial centres on the fringes of the Sahara such as
Sijilmasa, Wargla, and Timbuktu. From here it was made into
ingots, passed on to Marrakech, Tunis, Cairo, and Alexandria
where, as one Venetian merchant noted, 'it is bought by us

Italians and other Christians from the Moors with the various merchandize we give them'. A mixture of fact and fable, Cresques' map shows what Europe wanted from Africa at the end of the 14th century. It also emphasizes how Portugal was able to turn its previously marginal and isolated position on the western edge of Europe to full advantage. The Portuguese began settling the Atlantic islands of Madeira, the Canaries, and the Azores for commercial profit from the 1420s onwards. However, the Portuguese crown and merchants soon realized that seaborne travel along the African coastline could tap into the gold and spice trade at source. This could boldly circumvent taxes imposed on overland trade routes through Ottoman territories.

However, such an ambitious project involved organization and capital. By the mid-15th century German, Florentine, Genoese, and Venetian merchants were sponsoring Portuguese voyages down the coast of West Africa and offering the Portuguese king a percentage of any profits. Between 1454 and 1456 the Venetian merchant Alvise Cadamosto sailed down the coast of Africa, travelling via Cape Blanco up the Senegal River and then around Cape Verde (encompassing present-day Senegal and Gambia). Landing at Cape Blanco, his main interest was in the Arab traders who made up the trans-Saharan trade route throughout the interior:

> These are the men who go to the land of the Blacks, and also to our nearer Barbary [North Africa]. They are very numerous, and have many camels on which they carry brass and silver from Barbary and other things to Tanbutu [Timbuktu] and to the land of the Blacks. Thence they carry away gold and pepper, which they bring hither.

However, it was not only gold that flowed back into Europe through these complex African trade routes. While travelling through the kingdom of a chieftain called 'Budomel' in southern Senegal, Cadamosto traded seven horses 'which together had cost me originally about three hundred ducats' for 100 slaves. For the Venetian this was a casual, but highly profitable deal, based on an accepted exchange rate of nine to 14 slaves for one horse (it has been estimated that at this time Venice itself had a population of over 3,000 slaves). Writing in 1446, Cadamosto estimated that 'every year the Portuguese take from Arguim 1,000 slaves', individuals who were taken back to Lisbon and sold throughout Europe. This trade represents one of the darkest sides of the European Renaissance, and marked the beginnings of a trans-Atlantic slave trade that was to bring misery and suffering to millions of Africans over subsequent centuries, lasting long after the official abolition of slavery in 1834. It is sobering to note how the economies funding the great cultural achievements of the Renaissance were profiting by this unscrupulous trade in human lives.

The African gold, pepper, cloth, and slaves that flowed back into mainland Europe, alongside the merchandise imported from the east also sowed the seeds of a global geographical understanding of the early modern world. In 1492, on the eve of Columbus' first voyage to the New World, the German cloth merchant Martin Behaim created an object that encompassed the fusion of global economics and artistic innovation that was becoming increasingly characteristic of the time. What Behaim created was the first known terrestrial globe of the world (Fig. 5). Lavishly illustrated with over 1,100 place names and 48 miniatures of kings and rulers, Behaim's globe also contained detailed legends describing merchandise, commercial practices, and trade routes across the known world. More than just an

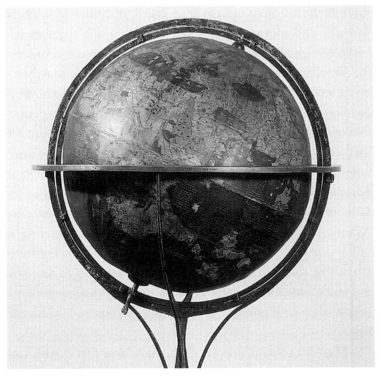

exquisite example of geographical scholarship, the globe was a commercial map of the Renaissance world, created by someone who was both a merchant and a geographer. Behaim recorded his own commercial experiences in West Africa between 1482 and 1484, and they give some indication of what motivated his voyages. He sailed 'with various goods and merchandise for sale and barter', including '18 horses with costly harness, to be presented to Moorish kings', as well as 'various examples of spices to be shown to the Moors in order that they might understand what we sought in their country'. Spices, gold, and slaves: these were the commodities that spurred the creation of the first truly global image of the early modern world.

Such cultural and commercial influences were not all one-way. One Portuguese chronicler noted 'in this kingdom of Kongo they make fabrics with a nap like velvet, some of them worked in velvety satin, so beautiful that nothing finer is made in Italy'. Another observed that, 'in Sierra Leone, men are very clever and make extremely beautiful objects such as spoons, saltcellars, and dagger hilts'. This is a direct reference to the remarkable carvings that have subsequently been called 'Afro-Portuguese ivories'. Carved by African artists from Sierra Leone and Nigeria, these beautiful art works fuse African style with European motifs to create a hybrid object that is unique to both cultures. Salt cellars and oliphants (hunting horns) were particularly common examples of such carvings, and were owned by figures as diverse as Albrecht Dürer and the Medici Family. One particularly striking salt cellar, dated to the early 16th century (Fig. 6), depicts four Portuguese figures supporting a basket upon which sails a Portuguese ship. With an added touch of humour a sailor peeps out from the crow's nest. The details of the clothing, weapons, and rigging are obviously drawn from detailed observation of and encounters with Portuguese seafarers. Scholars believe that these carvings were designed for export to Europe. They reveal a level of cultural interaction and exchange beyond traditional assumptions about Renaissance Europe's encounters with Africa. They also demonstrate that African design had a significant impact upon the art and architecture of the European Renaissance. The delicate beaded, braided, and twisted features of these carvings heavily influenced the architecture of 16th-century Portugal as it began to

raise monuments celebrating its commercial power in Africa and the Far East.

In 1492, as Behaim completed his globe and the craftsmen of Sierra Leone carved their ivories, Christopher Columbus set sail from Spain on a voyage into the western Atlantic. When Columbus landed in the Bahamas on 10 October 1492, he added another piece to Behaim's global jigsaw of the Renaissance, a 'New World' to the west. Within a century European geographers like Abraham Ortelius and Gerard Mercator were able to create a map of the world that looked strikingly modern. However, this assertion of European global dominance would prove to be anything but harmonious and 'civilizing' over the next five hundred years.

2. The humanist script

The indignity of man

In November 1466 George of Trebizond, one of the most celebrated humanist scholars of the 15th century, found himself lan-
guishing in a Roman jail on the orders of his employer, Pope Paul
II. Since his arrival in Venice as a Greek-speaking scholar, George
had established himself as a brilliant practitioner of the new
intellectual and educational arts of the day inspired by the classical authors of Greece and Rome. Utilizing his skills in Greek
and Latin, he rapidly rose to prominence with the publication of
textbooks on rhetoric and logic, and commentaries and translations of Aristotle and Plato. His reputation is recaptured in
an account of his presence at the Council of Florence in 1439,
where he:

> . . . lectured in public and in private, in his own house, in several
> subjects, and in Greek and Latin, and in logic and in philosophy; he
> produced a *Dialectics* so that his students could learn [logic], and like-
> wise he produced a *Rhetoric* which was much honoured. He used to
> give his students many exercises. At this time there was not in Flor-
> ence a more useful man than he for teaching, in addition to his
> learning and eloquence.

By 1450 George was papal secretary and leading lecturer in
the new humanities curriculum, the so-called *studia humanitatis*,
at the Studio Romano, under the patronage of Pope Nicholas V.
However, younger humanist scholars soon began criticizing
George's translations; they ran rival lecture courses and undermined his position in Rome. In 1465 George headed for

Mehmed the Conqueror's new capital of Istanbul, formerly Constantinople. Knowing Mehmed's scholarly interests, George wrote a preface to the classical Greek geographer Ptolemy that he dedicated to the sultan, 'thinking that there is nothing better in the present life than to serve a wise king and one who philosophizes about the greatest matters'. George also dedicated his comparison of Aristotle and Plato to the sultan, and returned to Rome to compose a series of letters to Mehmed, claiming that 'there has never been a man nor will there ever be one to whom God has granted a greater opportunity for sole dominion of the world'. In his rhetorically powerful letters and dedications George apparently saw Mehmed as a suitable patron of his academic skills. The pope wasn't impressed, and imprisoned George upon learning of his intellectual flirtation with the sultan. George's incarceration was brief, and after a stint in Budapest, he returned to Rome, where he witnessed his books on rhetoric and dialectic receive a new lease of life as a result of their distribution via a new invention: the printing press.

This chapter examines the rise of one of the most complex and controversial of all philosophical terms, Renaissance humanism, and its close relationship to one of the most important technological developments of the pre-modern world, the invention of the printing press. What united these two developments was the book. At the beginning of the 15th century, literacy and books were the preserve of a tiny, international elite focused on urban centres like Constantinople, Baghdad, Rome, and Venice. By the end of the 16th century humanism and the printing press had created a revolution in both elite and popular apprehensions of reading, writing, and the status of knowledge, transmitted via the printed book, which became focused much more exclusively on northern Europe.

George of Trebizond's career spans a defining moment for both intellectual thought and the history of the book. This was a time when a whole generation of intellectuals developed a new method of learning derived from classical Greek and Roman authors, called *studia humanitatis*. These scholars fashioned themselves 'humanists' and engaged in an immense undertaking to understand, translate, publish, and teach the texts of the past as a means of understanding and transforming their own present. Renaissance humanism gradually replaced the medieval scholastic tradition from which it emerged. It systematically promoted the study of classical works as the key to the creation of the successful, cultivated, civilized individual who used these skills to succeed within the everyday world of politics, trade, and religion.

Humanism's success lay in its claim to offer two things to its followers. Firstly, it fostered a belief that the mastery of the classics made you a better, more 'humane' person, able to reflect on the moral and ethical problems that the individual faced in relation to his/her social world. Secondly, it convinced its students and employers that the study of classical texts provided the practical skills necessary for a future career as an ambassador, lawyer, priest, or secretary within the layers of bureaucratic administration that began to emerge throughout 15th-century Europe. Humanist training in translation, letter-writing, and public speaking was viewed as a highly marketable education for those who wanted to enter the ranks of the social elite.

This sounds a long way from the romantic, idealized picture of humanism rescuing the great books of classical culture and absorbing their wisdom in creating a civilized society. It is. Renaissance humanism had a clearly pragmatic aim, namely to supply a framework for professional advancement, in particular to prepare men for government. A modern humanities education is constructed on the same model (the term is itself drawn from the Latin *studia humanitatis*). It promises the same benefits, and arguably retains the same flaws. It relies on the now completely accepted assumption that a non-vocational study of the liberal arts makes you a more civilized person, and gives you the linguistic and rhetorical skills required to succeed in the workplace. However, there are abiding tensions built into this assumption, tensions that can be traced back to the ideological practices of early Renaissance humanism: for instance, the contradiction between the inflated authority invested in the role of the teacher and the ideal of free-thinking, and the reality of rote-learning and intellectual conformity.

Many of these conflicts can be traced in the career of George of Trebizond. It reveals that the development of Renaissance humanism was an intellectually gruelling practical business that involved the painstaking detection, translation, editing, publication, and teaching of classical texts. George's combination of writing, translating, and teaching suggests that the success of humanism was mainly achieved within the classroom as a practical preparation for employment. New curricula and methods of teaching the demanding skills required of a humanist education were introduced. Humanism relied upon the creation of an academic community to teach and disseminate its ideas, but its members also quarrelled over the nature and direction of humanism's development, leading to the kind of vicious disputes and bitter rivalries that George experienced, and which compromised his career. Humanism marketed its skills to a governing elite that was persuaded to value the linguistic, rhetorical, and administrative expertise that a humanist education provided. However, this pragmatic promotion of humanism could often run into problems, as George discovered in his attempt to transfer his intellectual allegiance and humanistic skills from one powerful patron (Pope Paul II) to another (Mehmed the Conqueror). As a result, humanism concentrated its efforts on disseminating its method through the classroom and the revolutionary medium of the printing press. Humanism's alliance with print allowed scholars to distribute standardized copies of their publications in vast numbers way beyond the reproductive possibilities of scribal, manuscript production. The impact of this association was a subsequent rise in both literacy and schools, creating an unprecedented emphasis on education as a tool of socialization.

The persuaders

The story of Renaissance humanism begins with the 14th-century Italian writer and scholar Petrarch. He was closely associated with the papal residency in Avignon in France, where his father was employed as a notary—a scholar skilled in the art of administering the mass of documents created by papal business. Petrarch drew on these scholarly traditions in his interest in the rhetorical and stylistic qualities of a range of neglected classical Roman writers, particularly Cicero, Livy, and Virgil. He began piecing together texts like Livy's *History of Rome*, collating different manuscript fragments, correcting corruptions in the language, and imitating its style in writing a more linguistically fluent and rhetorically persuasive form of Latin.

Petrarch also scoured libraries and monasteries for classical texts, and in 1333 discovered a manuscript of the Roman statesman and orator Cicero's speech *Oration for Archias* (*Pro Archia*) that discussed the virtues of 'de studiis humanitatis'. Petrarch described the speech as 'full of wonderful compliments to poets'. Cicero was crucial to Petrarch and the subsequent development of humanism because he offered a new way of thinking about how the cultured individual united the philosophical and contemplative side of life with its more active and public dimension. In his famous text *On the Orator* (*De Oratore*), Cicero posed this problem by contrasting rhetoric and oratory with philosophy. For Cicero, 'the whole art of oratory lies open to the view, and is concerned in some measure with the common practice, custom, and speech of mankind'. Philosophy, on the other hand, involved private contemplation away 'from public interests', in fact divorced 'from any kind of business'. Petrarch took up Cicero's distinction in his treatise *The Solitary Life* (*De vita solitaria*) in his discussion of the role of the philosopher and the role of the orator:

> Both the diversity of their ways of life and the wholly opposed ends for which they have worked make me believe that philosophers have always thought differently from orators. For the latter's efforts are directed toward gaining the applause of the crowd, while the former strive—if their declarations are not false—to know themselves, to return the soul to itself, and to despise empty glory.

This was the blueprint for Petrarch's humanism: the unification of the philosophical quest for individual truth, and the more pragmatic ability to function effectively in society through the use of rhetoric and persuasion. To obtain the perfect balance the civilized individual needed rigorous training in the disciplines of the *studia humanitatis*, namely grammar, rhetoric, poetry, history, and moral philosophy.

This was a brilliant argument for giving the early humanist greater power and prestige than their scholastic predecessors had ever enjoyed. Medieval scholasticism had trained students in Latin, letter-writing and philosophy, but its teachers and thinkers were generally subservient to the authorities (usually the church) for which they worked. Cicero's definition of the civilized humanist, able to philosophize on humanity while also train the elite in the skills of public oratory and persuasion, gave humanism and its practitioners greater autonomy to 'sell' their ideas to social and political institutions. However, humanism was never an explicitly political movement, although some of its practitioners were quite happy to allow its approach to be appropriated by political ideologies as and where this proved beneficial, as will become clear.

One particularly important practitioner of 15th-century Renaissance humanism was Leonardo Bruni. His career included stints as papal secretary (1405) and chancellor of Florence (1410). He was instrumental in the revival of classical Greek, translating Aristotle, Plato, and Xenophon into Latin. Bruni paid homage to Petrarch as having 'restored to life the *studia humanitatis* when they were already extinct, and opened for us the path to show in what manner we could acquire learning'. One of Bruni's most famous treatises was his *Panegyric to the City of Florence*, written c.1400. It begins in classic Ciceronian fashion, claiming that 'Florence is of such a nature that a more distinguished or splendid city cannot be found on the entire earth . . . of such admirable excellence that no one can match his eloquence with it'. Here was Bruni displaying his rhetorical skills as a Ciceronian orator, conducting a formal exercise in rhetoric and dialectic (persuasion through argument).

Humanists styled themselves as orators and rhetoricians, gurus of style rather than politics. However, access to the corridors of political power was the oxygen upon which humanism thrived. Bruni's *Panegyric* should not be simply interpreted as an example of humanism's endorsement of the civic republican values of cities like Florence. It is often a mistake to take the subject matter of humanist writing at face value. Such writings were highly formal exercises in style and rhetoric, often delighting in dialectically arguing for and against a particular topic. The literary celebration of a city was just one of many stylistic exercises practised by Bruni and his humanist associates. Bruni presumably hoped that his *Panegyric* would assist his fortunes as a political functionary in Florence, but his translations of other texts show that he could quite comfortably support other political ideologies. In 1435 he completed a translation of Aristotle's *Politics* from the original Greek. He dedicated lavish presentation copies to Pope Eugenius IV and Alfonso, king of Aragon (both bitter political rivals). In his dedication to Alfonso he argued that Aristotle's text was a 'great and rich instrument for the government of a kingdom, and a proper implement for a king'. Humanism's triumph lay in its ability to utilize its skills in rhetoric, oratory, and dialectic to convince a range of potential political paymasters of the usefulness of its services, be they republican or monarchical.

Back to the drawing board

By the mid-15th century the practice of humanism was spreading throughout schools, universities, and courts. Its emphasis on rhetoric and language meant that the status of the book as a material and intellectual object took on new importance. Humanism's revisions of how to speak, translate, read, and even write Latin all focused on the book as the perfect portable object through which to disseminate these ideas. A later 15th-century manuscript copy of Diomedes' Latin *Grammatica* provides a good example of the kind of teaching text used by Renaissance teachers (Fig. 7). It is also written in the new humanist script: this replaced medieval Gothic script and, in its rejection of Gothic's abbreviations and fusion of letters, made text more accessible.

But how did these humanist ideals work in practice? The two illustrations at the bottom of Diomedes' *Grammatica* provide some insight into the gulf between humanism's intellectual claims and its reality. On the right is a scene from a typical Renaissance classroom: a humanist teacher lectures to a collection of rowdy boys. On the left, the same teacher's punishment involves giving one young boy's buttocks a worryingly energetic thrashing.

One particularly vivid example of this gulf between the theory of humanism and its practice in the classroom emerges from the career of one of the most respected of all humanist teachers, Guarino Guarini of Verona (1374–1460). Guarino studied Greek in Constantinople and returned to Italy in 1408 armed with a collection of Greek manuscripts with which he established a fearsome reputation as a translator, teacher, and lecturer. In 1429 he was employed by the Este dynasty in Ferrara, where he opened a famous school; this became the basis for the new arts faculty of the University of Ferrara, where Guarino lectured as Professor of Rhetoric from 1436.

Guarino's success as a teacher rested on his ability to sell to both his students and his patrons a vision of humanist education

7.
The humanist classroom, from a late 15th-century illuminated manuscript of Diomedes' *Grammatica*. Rowdiness and strict discipline were common features of Renaissance education.

that combined civilized humane values with practical social skills crucial to social advancement. In one introductory lecture on Cicero, Guarino asked rhetorically:

> What better goal can there be for our thoughts and efforts than the arts precepts and studies by which we come to guide, order and govern ourselves, our households and our political offices[?] . . . Therefore continue as you have begun, excellent youths and gentlemen, and work at these Ciceronian studies which fill our city with well-founded hope in you, and which bring honour and pleasure to you.

This is the ideology of Renaissance humanism. It was a vision disseminated by a group of teachers and scholars trained in the art of rhetoric and persuasion; no wonder it was accepted so readily in its day, and continues to be believed today.

However, Guarino's classroom did not necessarily produce the humane, elite citizens he promised. Guarino's education involved a gruelling immersion in grammar and rhetoric, based on diligent note-taking, rote learning of texts, oral repetition, and rhetorical imitation in a seemingly endless round of basic exercises. There was little time for more philosophical reflection on the nature of the texts under analysis, and students' lecture notes reveal only a very basic grasp of the new ways of speaking and writing that humanists like Guarino believed were the basis of humanist education. These elementary lessons in language and rhetoric did prepare students for basic employment in legal, political, and religious positions, although this was a far cry from the exalted heights promised by Guarino in his introductory lectures.

The approach Guarino advocated may also have had more insidious effects. His methods delighted his political patrons. The repetitious drilling of students in fine points of grammar cultivated passivity, obedience, and docility, and where this failed, discipline and correction of the sort represented in the illustration to Diomedes' *Grammatica*, seems to have been routinely implemented. Guarino also explicitly encouraged subservience towards the politics of the ruling elite, be they republican or (as in the case of his own patrons, the Este) monarchical:

> Whatever the ruler may decree must be accepted with a calm mind and the appearance of pleasure. For men who can do this are dear to rulers, make themselves and their relatives prosperous, and win high promotion.

For most humanist students, the rhetorical claims of humanism towards a new conception of the individual led in practice to employment in the foundations of the emerging political state. Guarino ensured that political acquiescence matched the practical skills required for such positions. This guaranteed ongoing elite sponsorship of schools and universities that disseminated the ideals of humanism.

A woman's place is in the humanist's home

From humanism's rhetoric of the dignity of humanity it might be expected that it also afforded new intellectual and social opportunities for women. In fact, humanism's relationship to women was far more ambivalent. In his treatise *On the Family* (1444), the Italian humanist Leon Battista Alberti defined a humanist vision of the domestic household, owned by men but run by women:

> the smaller household affairs, I leave to my wife's care ... it would hardly win us respect if our wife busied herself among the men in the marketplace, out in the public eye. It also seems somewhat demeaning to me to remain shut up in the house among women when I have

manly things to do among men, fellow citizens and worthy and distinguished foreigners.

Drawing on Cicero and the Greek writer Xenophon's *Oeconomicus*, Alberti created a highly influential vision of the sexual division of labour and the domestic economy of the household. The eloquent public man is contrasted with his silent, domestic wife, who remains 'locked up at home'. Her only training is in the running of the household. To ensure its successful maintenance, the husband reveals all its contents to his wife, with just one exception. Only 'my books and records' are kept locked away, and 'these my wife not only could not read, she could not lay hands on them'. Alberti is anxious at the thought 'of bold and forward females who try too hard to know about things outside the house and about the concerns of their husband and of men in general'.

Alberti's attitude influenced humanist responses to elite women who challenged their assigned role and pursued a vocation in humanist learning. Scholars like Leonardo Bruni did not completely reject women's pursuit of learning, but were adamant that it should only go so far. In an address written around 1405 to Battista Malatesta, the wife of Galeazzo Malatesta, Lord of Pesaro, Bruni cautioned that it 'is not at all admirable' for women to study geometry, arithmetic, astronomy, and even rhetoric, for 'why exhaust a woman with the concerns of *status*[?]' Learning rhetoric and the art of public speaking is particularly dangerous, because 'if a woman throws her arms around while speaking, or if she increases the volume of her speech with greater forcefulness, she will appear threateningly insane and require restraint'. Women could learn cultivation, decorum, and household skills, but formal expertise in applied subjects that could lead to public and professional visibility were frowned upon.

In spite of such hostility, learned women like Battista Malatesta, Christine de Pizan (*c*.1364–1431), Isotta Nogarola (1418–66), and Cassandra Fedele (1465–1558) did attempt to carve out intellectual careers. In *The Book of the City of Ladies* (1404–5) the French writer Christine de Pizan argued that 'those who blame women out of jealousy are those wicked men who have seen and perceived many women of greater intelligence and nobler conduct than they themselves possess'. In the 1430s Isotta Nogarola of Verona responded to attacks on women's loquaciousness by suggesting that 'rather than women exceeding men in talkativeness, in fact they exceed them in eloquence and virtue'. However, such forays into publishing and public speaking were regarded as novel events rather than professional activities. In 1438 Nogarola was viciously slandered by an anonymous pamphleteer for her attempt to 'speak out'. He conflated her learning with sexual promiscuity, declaiming with a heavy-handed double entendre that 'the woman of fluent tongue is never chaste'. Once a woman crossed the line from accomplished student to orator in the public sphere, the humanist response was to either castigate her for being sexually aggressive, or mystify and trivialize women's intellectual dialogue as amorous exchanges between lovers.

Renaissance humanism did not create new opportunities for women; it just changed the conditions under which they experienced social oppression. It encouraged women's education as a social adornment and an end in itself, not as a means to step out of the household and into the public sphere. Struggling male humanist teachers and students were having enough difficulty carving out their own public and professional positions. The possibility of women achieving such a public profile was clearly threatening, potentially embarrassing, and ultimately intolerable.

However, the rhetoric of Renaissance humanism extolled the virtues of education and eloquence, and wherever possible women attempted to take advantage of the opportunities afforded by these developments. If women did have a Renaissance, it was usually in spite of their male humanist counterparts.

The printing press: a revolution in communication

In the mid-1460s, as scholars and teachers like George of Trebizond and Guarino came to the end of their careers, Alberti wrote that he 'approved very warmly of the German inventor who has recently made it possible, by making certain imprints of letters, for three men to make more than two hundred copies of a given original text in one hundred days, since each pressing yields a page in large format'. It is no surprise that a scholar like Alberti should embrace the invention of the printing press. The invention of movable type in Germany around 1450 was the most important technological and cultural innovation of the Renaissance. Humanism was quick to see the practical possibilities of utilizing a medium of mass reproduction, as Alberti suggests, but the revolutionary effect of print was most pronounced in northern Europe.

The invention of printing emerged from a commercial and technological collaboration between Johann Gutenberg, Johann Fust, and Peter Schöffer in Mainz in the early 1450s. Their different backgrounds reveal much of the nature of early printing. Gutenberg was a goldsmith, who adapted his expertise in metalwork to cast moveable metal type for the press. Schöffer was a copyist and calligrapher, who used his skills in copying manuscripts to design, compose, and set the printed text. Fust provided the finance required. Printing was a collaborative process, and primarily a commercial business run by entrepreneurs for profit. Drawing on the much earlier eastern inventions of the woodcut and paper, Gutenberg and his team printed a Latin Bible in 1455 and in 1457 issued an edition of the Psalms.

According to Schöffer printing was simply 'the art of writing artificially without reed or pen'. At first, the new medium didn't grasp its own significance. Many early printed books used scribes trained in manuscript illumination to imitate the unique appearance of manuscripts, producing opulent books like Aristotle's *Works* (Plate 4). Published in Venice in 1483, the text is surrounded by exquisitely painted scenes of satyrs, fantastic landscapes, monuments, and fabulous jewels. The printed page itself is disguised as torn and peeling parchment, while above Aristotle debates with his Muslim translator and commentator, the philosopher Averroës. The opulent decoration of these half-painted, half-printed books suggests that they were regarded as precious commodities in their own right, valued as much for their appearance as their content. Wealthy patrons like Isabella d'Este, Mehmed the Conqueror, and Federico da Montefeltro invested heavily in this type of printed book that sat alongside their more traditional manuscripts.

However, it soon became clear that print offered distinct advantages over manuscripts. The blighted career of the Florentine bookseller Vespasiano da Bisticci is a prime example of the shift in sheer numbers of books that came with the invention of printing. Bisticci was one of the most successful manuscript publishers and booksellers in mid-15th-century Italy, supplying books to patrons as diverse as Federico da Montefeltro, the Duke of Urbino, King Matthias Corvinus of Hungary, and John Tiptoft,

Earl of Worcester. Vespasiano wildly exaggerated in claiming that he constructed a library for Cosimo de' Medici in the 1460s by employing 45 scribes, who copied 200 manuscripts in two years. This compares to the output of the German printers Sweynheym and Pannartz, who established the first Italian printing press in Rome in 1465. In their first five years they printed 12,000 books. Vespasiano would have needed over 100 scribes to copy the same number of manuscripts. By the 1480s the disillusioned Vespasiano was driven out of business, by which time more than 100 printing presses were at work throughout Italy.

Print became unstoppable. By 1480 printing presses had been successfully established in all the major cities of Germany, France, the Netherlands, England, Spain, Hungary, and Poland. It has been estimated that by 1500 these presses had printed between six and 15 million books in 40,000 different editions, more books than had been produced since the fall of the Roman Empire. The figures for the 16th century are even more startling. In England alone 10,000 editions were printed and at least 150 million books were published amongst a European population of fewer than 80 million people.

The consequence of this massive dissemination of print was a revolution in knowledge and communication that affected society from top to bottom. The speed and quantity with which books were distributed suggests that print cultivated new communities of readers eager to consume the diverse material that rolled off the presses. The accessibility and relatively low cost of printed books also meant that more people than ever before had access to books. Printing was a profitable business. It responded to public demand, and the success and wealth of the great printing houses of Manutius and Jensen in Venice, Caxton in London, and

Plantin in Antwerp suggests that this demand was substantial. As more people spoke and wrote in the European vernacular languages—German, French, Italian, Spanish, and English—the printing presses increasingly published these languages rather than Latin and Greek, which appealed to a smaller audience. Vernacular languages were gradually standardized, and became the primary means of legal, political, and literary communication in most European states. This encouraged the rise of national consciousness. The mass of printed books in everyday languages contributed to the image of a national community amongst those who shared a common vernacular. Over the centuries this would ultimately lead to individuals defining themselves in relation to a nation rather than a religion or ruler, a situation which had profound consequences for religious authority, with the erosion of the absolute authority of the Catholic Church and the rise of a more secular form of Protestantism.

Printing permeated every area of public and private life. Initially presses issued religious books—bibles, breviaries, sermons, and catechisms—but gradually more secular books were introduced, like romances, travel narratives, pamphlets, broadsheets, and conduct books advising people on everything from medicine to wifely duties. By the 1530s, printed pamphlets sold for the same price as a loaf of bread, while a copy of the New Testament cost the same as a labourer's daily wage. A culture based on communication through listening, looking, and speaking gradually changed into a culture that interacted through reading and writing. Rather than being focused on courts or churches, a literary culture began to emerge around the semi-autonomous printing press. Its agenda was set by demand and profit rather than religious orthodoxy or political ideology. Printing houses turned intellectual and cultural creativity into a collaborative venture, as printers, merchants, teachers, scribes, translators, artists, and writers all pooled their skills and resources in creating the finished product. One print historian has compared the late 15th-century Venetian printing press of Aldus Manutius to a sweatshop, boarding house, and research institute all in one. Presses like Manutius' created an international community of printers, financiers, and writers, as opportunities for expansion into new markets emerged.

Print also transformed how knowledge itself was understood and transmitted. A manuscript is a unique and unreproducible object, however brilliant its copyist. Print, however, with its standard format and type, introduced exact mass reproduction. This meant that two readers separated by distance could discuss and compare identical books, right down to a specific word on a particular page. With the introduction of consistent pagination, indexes, alphabetic ordering, and bibliographies (all unthinkable in manuscripts), knowledge itself was slowly repackaged. Textual scholarship became a cumulative science, as scholars could now gather manuscripts of, say, Aristotle's *Politics* and print a standard authoritative edition based on a comparison of all available copies. This also led to the phenomenon of new and revised editions. Publishers realized the possibility of incorporating discoveries and corrections into the collected works of an author. As well as being intellectually rigorous, this was also commercially very profitable, as individuals could be encouraged to buy a new version of a book they already possessed. Pioneering reference books and encyclopaedias on subjects like language and law claimed to reclassify knowledge according to new methodologies of alphabetical and chronological order.

The printing press did not just publish written texts. Part of the revolutionary impact of print was the creation of what William Ivins has called 'the exactly repeatable pictorial statement'. Using woodcuts and the more sophisticated technique of copperplate engraving, printing made possible the mass diffusion of standardized images of maps, scientific tables and diagrams, architectural plans, medical drawings, cartoons, and religious images. At one end of the social scale visually arresting printed images had a huge impact upon the illiterate, especially when they were used for religious purposes. At the other end, exactly reproducible images revolutionized the study of subjects like geography, astronomy, botany, anatomy, and mathematics. The invention of printing sparked a communications revolution whose impact would be felt for centuries, and which would only be matched by the development of the internet and the revolution in information technology that took place at the end of the 20th century.

The humanist press

Humanists quickly realized the power of the printing press for spreading their own message. The most famous northern European humanist, Desiderius Erasmus of Rotterdam (1466–1536), used the printing press as a way of distributing his own particular brand of humanism, and in the process self-consciously styling himself as the 'Prince of Humanism'. Ordained as a priest, he received papal dispensation to pursue a career as an itinerant scholar and teacher, attaching himself to elite households and powerful printing firms throughout Europe. Responding to claims that the early humanists were more interested in classical

pagan writers than Christianity, Erasmus embarked on a career
of biblical translation and commentary that culminated in his
edition of the Greek New Testament with a facing Latin translation (1516). His enormously prolific output embraced translations and commentaries on the classics (including Seneca and
Plutarch), collections of Latin proverbs, treatises on language
and education, and copious letters to friends, printers, scholars,
and rulers across Europe. His most widely read book today is his
sardonic *Praise of Folly* (1511). This is a 'biting satire' that is
particularly scathing in its attack upon the corruption and
complacency of the church, which is characterized as believing
that 'teaching the people is hard work, prayer is boring, tears are
weak and womanish, poverty is degrading, and meekness is
disgraceful'.

Most of Erasmus' formidable intellectual energy went into
constructing an enduring scholarly community and educational
method, at the centre of which stood his own printed writings
and status as the ultimate 'man of letters'. The printing press was
central to Erasmus' astute manipulation of his intellectual career,
right down to the circulation of his own image. In 1526, after
much prompting from Erasmus, Dürer agreed to execute a
monumental engraving of him (Fig. 8). It shows Erasmus skilfully using this new printing technique to distribute a powerful,
commemorative image of the humanist scholar in his study,
writing letters and surrounded by his printed books, which as
Dürer's Greek inscription suggests, represent Erasmus' lasting
fame: 'His works will give a better image of him'.

In 1512 Erasmus published one of his most influential works,
De Copia, a textbook of exercises in the eloquent expression
of Latin. Most famously it contains 200 ways to express the

IMAGO · ERASMI·ROTERODA-
MI · AB · ALBERTO · DVRERO·AD
VIVAM· EFFIGIEM· DELINIATA·

THN·KPEITTΩ·TA·ΣYΓΓPAM
MATA·ΔΙΞEI

·MDXXVI·

8.
Dürer's
monumental
portrait of
Erasmus, engraved
in 1526, and
circulated
throughout Europe
as a way of
establishing
Erasmus'
reputation as the
great humanist
intellectual.

sentiment 'As long as I live, I shall preserve the memory of you.'
The title page of the first edition (Fig. 9), with its depiction of the
busy printing house and the screw press, captures how important
the press was for Erasmus. *De Copia* was written for his friend

D. Erasmi Roterodami de dupli
ci Copia rerū ac verborū commentarii duo.
De ratione studii & instituendi pueros commentarii totidē.
De puero Iesu Concio scholastica:& Quædam carmina ad eandem rem per
tinentia.

Prelū Ascēsianū

Venundantur in ædibus Ascensianis.

John Colet, dean of St Paul's School in London. In his dedication
to Colet, Erasmus claimed that he wanted 'to make a small literary contribution to the equipment of your school', choosing

'these two new commentaries *De Copia*, inasmuch as the work in question is suitable for boys to read'. Here was Erasmus cleverly marketing his new humanist curriculum through the medium of the printing press. Subsequent editions of *De Copia* were dedicated to influential European scholars and patrons, to ensure that the book was used not just in London but also in classrooms across Europe. Erasmus realized that he needed to build on the scholarly achievements of 15th-century humanism by using the medium of print to market a whole new way of learning and living. He combined classical and Christian learning with the construction of a methodical humanist curriculum in the circulation of books as diverse as his *New Testament* and *De Copia*.

Erasmus also appreciated that as well as revolutionizing the classroom, humanism had to ingratiate itself with political authority. In 1516 he composed his *Education of a Christian Prince* and dedicated it to a Hapsburg prince, the future Emperor Charles V. This was an advice manual for the young prince in how to exercise 'absolute rule over free and willing subjects', and the need for education and advice from those skilled in philosophy and rhetoric. In other words, Erasmus was making a bid for public office as the young prince's personal adviser and public relations guru. Although Charles graciously accepted the manual, no position was forthcoming. Erasmus' response was to send another copy of *Education of a Christian Prince* to Charles's political rival, King Henry VIII! In his dedication written in 1517 Erasmus praised Henry as a king who managed to 'devote some portion of your time to reading books', which Erasmus argued made Henry 'a better man and a better king'. Erasmus tried to convince Henry that the pursuit of humanism was the best way to run his kingdom, suggesting that it would make him a better person, and provide the skills necessary to achieve his political ends. It is significant that Erasmus felt it appropriate to dedicate the same text to both Charles V and Henry VIII. He presumed that both sovereigns would get the point that he could use his rhetorical skills to construct whatever political argument they required. If Erasmus could think up 200 ways of preserving a friend's memory, then he could be equally eloquent in justifying the actions of a sovereign—but only for a price.

Erasmus did not receive the lucrative political position that he coveted, but his dedication of the *Education* to Henry VIII did enhance his reputation in the Tudor corridors of power. Henry, like his political rivals Charles V, Francis I, John III of Portugal, and Sultan Süleyman the Magnificent, became convinced of the need to employ the expertise of humanist scholars. Diplomatic exchanges between east and west, as well as between the polyglot empires of western Europe, required eloquence in both Greek and Latin, the preferred languages of international diplomacy. As the scale and complexity of these exchanges increased, the drafting of complex legal and political documents, mastery of public speaking and ambassadorial business, and an ability to discourse (and often dissimulate) on issues of politics, religion, and business became prized skills. By the 1530s Henry was in particular need of the rhetorical skills of Erasmus and his followers. The king was eager to justify divorcing his first wife, Catherine of Aragon, to allow him to marry Anne Boleyn. However, the Pope refused to sanction the divorce. Henry's challenge to papal authority started to make him look dangerously like the Protestant reformer Martin Luther. In this situation of extreme political sensitivity, Henry's response was to employ a team of academic experts, all trained humanists and followers of Erasmus, to build a case to justify his divorce, distance him from Luther, and support the subsequent concentration of absolute political and religious authority in his hands. Henry's secret marriage to Anne Boleyn, divorce from Catherine, and his establishment as head of the new Church of England represented the triumph of his political strategy, as well as the successful deployment of the rhetorical and intellectual skills provided by his resident humanists.

The politics of humanism

Out of these expedient collaborations between humanism and politics emerged two of the most influential books in the history of political theory and business management: Niccolò Machiavelli's *The Prince* (1513) and Thomas More's *Utopia* (1516). Today both books are still often read as timeless classics of how to maintain political power and create ideal societies. They are in fact highly specific products of both writers' experience of the relationship between humanism and politics in the first half of the 16th century.

Machiavelli's book was written in the wake of the collapse of the Florentine republican government in 1512 and the return to power of the autocratic Medici family. A trained humanist, Machiavelli had served the republic for 14 years, before being dismissed and briefly imprisoned by the returning Medici. The intention of *The Prince* was to draw on his political experiences 'to discuss princely government, and to lay down rules about it'. What followed was a devastating account of how rulers should obtain and maintain power. Machiavelli concluded that if his suggestions were 'put into practice skilfully, they will make a new ruler seem very well established, and will quickly make his power more secure'. Machiavelli's background of humanist training and direct political experience produced a series of infamous pronouncements that drew on classical authors as well as contemporary political events. A 'ruler who wishes to maintain his power must be prepared to act immorally'; he should 'be a great feigner and dissembler', ready to 'act treacherously, ruthlessly, or inhumanely, and disregard the precepts of religion' in the interest of retaining political power.

Just like Erasmus' *Education of a Christian Prince*, Machiavelli's book was written as a bid for political employment (or in Machiavelli's case, re-employment). *The Prince* was dedicated to Giuliano de' Medici, the new autocratic ruler of Florence, and was referred to by its author as a 'token of my readiness to serve you'. Machiavelli admitted in his letters 'my desire that these Medici rulers should begin to use me'. *The Prince* was Machiavelli's attempt to offer pragmatic advice to the Medici on how to hold on to absolute political power. Machiavelli was taking Renaissance humanism to its logical political conclusion in providing his new ruler with the most persuasive and realistic account of how to retain power available. Machiavelli's humanism was prepared to market whatever political ideology was in control, be it autocratic or democratic. The tragedy for Machiavelli was that the Medici were unconvinced by his protestations of loyalty. He never attained high political office again, and *The Prince* remained unprinted at the time of his death in 1527.

Thomas More's *Utopia: Concerning the Best State of a Commonwealth and the New Island of Utopia* was also closely connected to its author's public career. A close friend of Erasmus and gifted student of law and Greek, More translated Lucian and wrote English and Latin poetry. In 1517 he entered Henry VIII's political council and became Lord Chancellor in 1529, ghost-writing many of Henry's political and theological tracts in the process. More exemplified Cicero's vision of the cultivated humanist—someone capable of accommodating private philosophical meditation with public oratory and involvement in the civic world of politics and diplomacy.

This delicate balancing act permeates *Utopia*. The book was written in the form of a Latin dialogue between learned men, in direct imitation of Plato's fashionable treatise on an ideal state, the *Republic*. It opens with More himself in Antwerp acting as Henry VIII's diplomatic representative. More's friend introduces him to Raphael Hythloday, an adventurer recently returned from the island of Utopia. Hythloday offers a detailed description of the ideal 'commonwealth' of Utopia, where 'all things are held in common', 'no men are beggars', and divorce, euthanasia, and public health are taken for granted.

Did More believe in his fictionalized vision of an ideal society? There are several reasons for believing that he was far more ambivalent about Utopia than many people have assumed. The word 'utopia' is a pun, a linguistic invention from the Greek that can either mean 'fortunate place' or 'no place'. Hythloday's name also means 'expert in nonsense'. More found many of Utopia's 'laws and customs' 'really absurd', but confessed 'that in the Utopian commonwealth there are many features in our own societies I would like rather than expect to see'. These are hardly ringing endorsements of his imaginary society.

Throughout the book, More refuses to endorse or condemn the politically contentious issues he discusses, from private property and religious authority to public office and philosophical speculation. This was not because he could not make up his mind: politically, he could not be seen to endorse a particular standpoint. As a skilled political counsellor More had to display his rhetorical skills in justifying often mutually incompatible or contradictory statements and beliefs in the service of the state. Utopia is not a society towards which More wishes to strive. It is a canvas upon which he can debate a range of issues relevant to his own particular world. If his analysis was ever called into question, he could always point out that he argued for the contrary position, or that Utopia was, after all, simply made up: it was nowhere.

Utopia advertises More's ability to eloquently discourse on a range of contentious issues that affected his employer, and upon which he was expected to advise. Unlike Machiavelli, More wrote *Utopia* at the height of his public career and had to be far more circumspect and politically flexible in his thinking. This is why the argument and style of *Utopia* is so ambivalent. The unemployed Machiavelli could offer a much less ambiguous and far more politically realistic account of politics and power in *The Prince*. More's refusal to endorse Henry's divorce was less a principled ethical position than a political miscalculation made on the grounds of religion, leading as it did to More's execution. Both his *Utopia* and Machiavelli's *The Prince* exhibit the political opportunism of the Renaissance humanist.

From Petrarch to More, Renaissance humanism flexibly served whoever it seemed politically expedient to follow, be they democratic or autocratic. This is why virtually every modern political philosophy from fascism to communism has claimed that books like *The Prince* and *Utopia* justify their own claims to power and authority. Renaissance humanism continues to exercise a powerful influence upon the modern humanities, but as this chapter has argued, humanism is not the idealized celebration of humaneness that it often claimed to be, but has a hard core of pragmatism. The legacy of Renaissance humanism is far more ambivalent than many have been led to believe, partly because its rhetoric remains so seductive.

3. Church and state

A political donation

In 1435 the humanist scholar Lorenzo Valla arrived in Naples to offer his services to its future king, Alfonso of Aragon. At the time Alfonso was locked in a political struggle with Pope Eugenius IV over possession of Naples. In typical humanist fashion, Valla went to work on a text of direct political relevance to his new paymaster: the *Donation of Constantine*. The *Donation* was one of the founding documents of the Roman Catholic Church. It purported to be a grant issued in the 4th century by the Emperor Constantine that granted sweeping imperial and territorial powers to the papacy. It was one of the most powerful and convincing justifications of papal claims to worldly authority. However, Valla exposed the *Donation* as a fake. Using his humanist skills in rhetoric, philosophy, and philology, he demonstrated that its historical anachronisms, philological errors, and contradictions in logic revealed that the *Donation* was an 8th-century forgery.

The deftness of Valla's textual analysis was matched by his scathing attack upon the Roman Church and its pontiffs, who had either 'not known that the *Donation of Constantine* is spurious and forged, or else they forged it'. He accused them of 'dishonouring the Christian religion, confounding everything with murders, disasters and crimes'. Asking in typically polemical fashion, 'which shall I censure more, the stupidity of the ideas, or of the words?', Valla ridiculed the inaccurate and anachronistic Latin of the *Donation*, before again posing the rhetorical question 'can we justify the principle of papal power when we perceive it to be the cause of such great crimes and of such great and varied evils?' This rhetorically elegant invective concluded with an attack upon the imperial pretensions of the Pope, who, 'so that he may recover the other parts of the *Donation*, money wickedly stolen from good people he spends more wickedly'. Alfonso was delighted with Valla's demolition of the *Donation* and used its arguments in his ultimately successful attempt to secure the kingdom of Naples despite concerted papal opposition.

The story of Valla's revelation represents a new development in the relations between Renaissance religion, politics, and learning. The rise of political organizations like the sovereign state created the need for new intellectual and administrative skills required for organizing political structures and successfully challenging the authority of institutions like the church. The fact that Pope Martin V subsequently employed Valla as a papal secretary may seem surprising in the light of his exposure of the *Donation*. However, it reveals the church's pragmatic attitude towards such scholars (better the devil you know). It also shows how politically strategic humanists like Valla were prepared to be when new opportunities beckoned.

This story is pivotal to understanding the complex interrelation of the topics central to this chapter: the religion and politics of the Renaissance. Between 1400 and 1600 religious belief was an integral part of everyday life. It was also impossible to separate religion from the practice of political authority, the world of international finance, and the achievements of art and learning. As the Catholic Church struggled to assert its temporal and spiritual power throughout this period, it faced perpetual conflict, dissent, and division. This culminated in the Reformation that

swept through 16th-century northern Europe, creating the greatest crisis in the history of the Roman Church. The Catholic
Counter-Reformation of the mid-16th century transformed the
Church forever and, combined with the Protestant Reformation
led by Martin Luther, established the general shape of Christianity as it exists today in Europe. The Reformation also raised even
more complex questions concerning Christianity's relationship
with the other two great religions of the book, Judaism and Islam,
both of which asserted their theological superiority over Christianity, and which in the case of Islam was quick to exploit the
schisms of the 16th-century Christian church. Despite the claims
of many church historians, the church was not triumphant in the
Renaissance. On the contrary, it was in perpetual crisis. Doubt,
anxiety, and inward contemplation remain cornerstones of modern thinking and subjectivity, and their origins can be traced back
to the religious ferment of the period 1400–1600.

The other development that transformed religious authority
within this period was the rise of new forms of political authority.
From the late 15th century secular political organizations increasingly came to control the everyday lives of most people. The
wealth and administrative innovation that accompanied the
uneven commercial and urban expansion of the 15th century created the conditions for significant political upheaval and expansion. Italian cities like Florence and Venice experimented with
republican governments, and the courts of Milan, Naples,
Urbino, and Ferrara sought to expand their military and political
power bases through astute use of art, culture, learning, and
papal authority. In the north, the peace and prosperity that
followed the conclusion of the Hundred Years War in 1453 intensified the concentration of commercial wealth and sovereign

power in France and the territories of the Low Countries, predominantly controlled by the Hapsburg dynasty. To the east, the rise of the Ottoman Empire also provided central Europe with a model of imperial power with which to compete. By the middle of the 16th century, Europe was in the control of a series of sovereign states and empires—France, England, Portugal, Spain, and the Turks—that had effectively annexed the worldly power of religion. The rise of nation states and empires in the 16th century was in inverse proportion to the decline of the worldly power of the church. While many historians have celebrated this shift, the more baleful effects of nationalism and imperialism in the modern world reveal a more ambivalent side to this legacy of the Renaissance.

The revolting cardinals

By the beginning of the 15th century, the Catholic Church was in disarray. The word 'Catholic' came from the Greek word for 'universal', but by 1400 the church looked anything but universal. It had already experienced a traumatic division with its separation into the western, Roman church and the eastern, Orthodox church based in Constantinople in 1054. This was the result of theological and territorial differences that had been growing since Constantine's settlement of Constantinople as the new centre of the Roman Empire in 330. Over the following three centuries the church battled to assert its theological and imperial authority in the face of opposition from inside and outside. The pope claimed by biblical authority that, as Christ's representative on earth, he held political sway over worldly issues: 'I will give you the keys of the kingdom of heaven, and whatever you bind on earth shall be bound in heaven and whatever you loose on earth shall be loosed in heaven' (Matthew 16: 19).

In 1309 under pressure from the French crown the papacy moved to Avignon in southern France. By 1377 it had returned to Rome, but only to see a rival French pope elected the following year and reinstalled in Avignon. The Papal Schism allowed dissident cardinals from both sides to propose what became known as the conciliar theory of church governance. This led church councils to impose their collective authority over unacceptable and (in this case) schismatic popes. In 1409 the Council of Pisa declared both the Avignon and Roman popes heretical, and elected a new pope. However, his authority was ignored, and Christianity was left in the ignominious position of trying to accommodate three popes.

In 1414 the church fathers convened the Council of Constance to put an end to the Schism. It was an extraordinary event that lasted for three years. It attracted no less than two popes, one king, 32 princes, 47 archbishops, 361 lawyers, 1,500 knights, 1,400 merchants, 5,000 priests, and 700 prostitutes amongst its 72,000 attendants. The Council ruled that 'all men, of every rank and condition, including the pope himself, are bound to obey it in matters concerning the Faith, the abolition of the schism, and the reformation of the Church of God'. This allowed the Council to end the schism in 1417 by appointing Martin V as the first uncontested Roman pope for nearly a century. However, the Council also retained its authoritarian dimension. Both the English Lollards and the Bohemian Hussites were condemned as heretical for their popular condemnation of the sale of indulgences, calls for vernacular translations of the Bible, and free preaching of the gospel. In 1415 John Huss was burned at the stake at the behest of the Council for refusing to renounce these beliefs. The Council successfully concentrated religious power in the hands of one pope, based in Rome, but it also stirred up popular calls for religious reform that would return to haunt the church.

An orthodox marriage

In flexing its muscle and crushing the Papal Schism, the Council of Constance had unintentionally increased the autocratic power of the pope. Both Pope Martin V and his successor, Eugenius IV, consolidated their authority by embarking on ambitious plans to rebuild Rome and unify with the Eastern Orthodox Church. In 1437 Eugenius dissolved the radical Council of Basle and ordered its removal to first Ferrara and then Florence to discuss the unification of the Eastern Orthodox and Western Roman churches. This cleverly deflected the Council's attempts to reduce papal authority even further, while heightening the pope's stature as a diplomatic power-broker on the international stage.

In February 1438 the Byzantine Emperor John VIII Paleologus arrived in Florence with a retinue of 700 Greeks and the head of the Orthodox Church, the Patriarch Joseph II. As well as the Greek delegation, deputations arrived from Trebizond, Russia, Armenia, Cairo, and Ethiopia. As with many Renaissance transactions ostensibly concerned with religion, this momentous official meeting between east and west had profound political and cultural implications. John VIII had proposed a union between the eastern and western branches of Christendom as the only realistic way to prevent the collapse of the Byzantine Empire and the capture of Constantinople in the face of the inexorable rise of the Ottoman Empire. The pope was eager to unify the two churches as a way of extending his own political power throughout Italy, as well as avoiding the more pressing internal disputes that had dogged him throughout the Council of Basle.

Away from official council business, delegates enthusiastically explored each other's intellectual and cultural achievements. The Greeks admired the architectural achievements of Brunelleschi, the sculpture of Donatello, and the frescoes of Masaccio and Fra Angelico. The Florentines marvelled at the extraordinary collection of classical books that John VIII and his scholarly retinue had brought with them from Constantinople. These included beautiful manuscripts of Plato, Aristotle, Plutarch, Euclid, and Ptolemy and other classical texts which were 'not accessible here' in Italy according to one envious scholar. The Egyptian delegation presented the Pope with a 10th-century Arabic manuscript of the Gospels translated from a Coptic original, and the Armenian delegation left behind 13th-century illuminated manuscripts on the Armenian Church that reflected its mixed Mongol, Christian, and Islamic heritage. The Ethiopian delegation also circulated elegant 15th-century Psalters written in Ethiopic and used in churches throughout northern and eastern Africa (Fig. 10).

These rich cultural exchanges between east and west also produced their own highly specific art objects that fused politics and religion. In 1438 Antonio Pisanello issued a portrait medal of John VIII Paleologus (Fig. 11) to commemorate the projected success of the unification of the two churches. The obverse shows John's profile, with peaked Byzantine hat and forked beard, while the reverse shows the emperor hunting. Such medals had circulated throughout the Roman and Byzantine

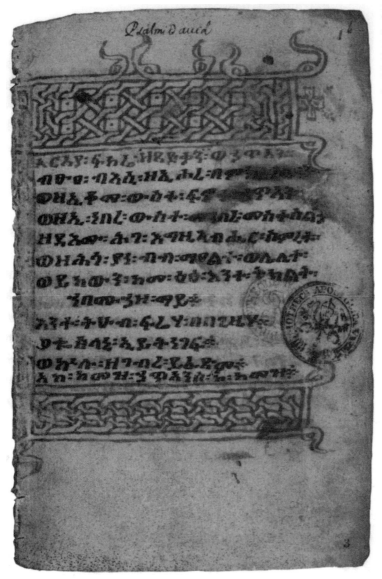

10.
The first psalm
from a 15th-century
Ethiopian Psalter,
just one of the
many eastern texts
brought to the
Council of
Florence in 1438.

11.
Pisanello's medal
of the Byzantine
Emperor John VIII
Paleologus. Made
in 1438 to
commemorate the
Council of
Florence, this was
the first portrait
medal made since
antiquity.

empires, but Pisanello's medal was the first of its kind to be cast in the Renaissance. The Byzantine scholars presumably supplied the idea for the medal, while Pisanello provided the skill required for its execution. Here again the east provides the inspiration for an artistic innovation that appears quintessentially 'Renaissance'. The power of the portrait medal was clearly felt in both the east and the west, which explains the creation of no less than three subsequent portrait medals of Mehmed the Conqueror (Fig. 20) once he took John VIII's place as ruler of Constantinople in 1453.

This portrait medal was not the only art object to emerge from the Council of Florence. Twenty years after the council, Benozzo Gozzoli completed his frescoes in the Palazzo Medici that celebrated the Medici's role in bringing together the eastern and western churches (Fig. 12). In Gozzoli's frescoes John VIII,

12.
Benozzo Gozzoli's lavish fresco *The Adoration of the Magi*: an artistic attempt by the Medici Bank to take the credit for bringing together eastern and western churches in 1438.

Joseph II, and Lorenzo de' Medici have become the three Magi. For political reasons Lorenzo's father, Cosimo de' Medici, had bankrolled the entire Council. The Medici had been negotiating commercial access to Constantinople throughout the 1430s, but an agreement was only reached in August 1439 as a token of John VIII's thanks for Cosimo's lavish hospitality throughout the Council of Florence. Cosimo's pious act of financial sacrifice for the good of the church was actually a ruthless sleight of hand. Eugenius remained even more financially indebted to the Medici, and Gozzoli's frescoes make it clear that the family regarded their involvement in unifying the two churches as even more important than the mediation of the pope.

On 6 July 1439 the Decree of Union was finally signed between the two churches. It rejoiced that 'the wall which separated the Eastern Church and the Western Church has been destroyed, and peace and concord have returned through "Christ the corner-stone who has made the two one" (Eph. 2:20,14), the most powerful bond of peace joining them and attaching them by a treaty of perpetual unity'. The rejoicing was short-lived. Back in Constantinople, the union was firmly rejected by the populace, stirred up by hardline orthodox members of the Eastern Church, while the Italian states demonstrated their reluctance by consistently refusing to provide military aid to assist the Byzantines in their struggle against the Ottomans. With the fall of Constantinople to Mehmed II in May 1453, the union came to a bloody and ignominious end.

The Council of Florence was a defining moment of the Renaissance. As a religious summit, it was a failure, crushing the papacy's hopes for the consolidation of its own imperial power through unification with the Eastern Church. As a political and cultural event, it was a triumph. It allowed the Italian states to challenge the authority of a weakened papacy, and strengthen its commercial relations to the east. Ruling families like the Medici cleverly manipulated their own role in the Council through sumptuous art objects like Gozzoli's frescoes that claimed Medicean pre-eminence in bringing about the Decree of Union. Culturally, the transmission of classical texts, ideas, and art objects from east to west that took place at the Council was to have a decisive effect on the art and scholarship of late 15th-century Italy.

The masses

What of the everyday reality of religious observance for the millions of people across Europe who regularly attended church and identified themselves as Christians? It would be idealistic to believe that debates about papal authority and textual exegesis had much impact upon many of these people. The church was part of the fabric of everyday life for most individuals, and this meant that the distinction between the sacred and the profane often became blurred. Churches were used for festivals, political meetings, eating, horse-trading, and even storing merchant's goods and valuables. The clergy were everywhere. By 1550 out of a population of 60,000, Florence boasted over 5,000 clergymen. Poorly educated and badly paid, they were often to be found working as masons, horse dealers, and cattle traders, keeping lovers and children, and carrying weapons.

In theory, the Catholic Church acted as the earthly manifestation of Christ's incarnation. It mediated between God and the individual, and was exclusively responsible for dispensing God's grace through the sacraments—baptism, confirmation, the Eucharist, penance, ordination, marriage, and extreme unction. According to the theory of transubstantiation, the priest possessed the miraculous (arguably magical) power of transforming the bread and wine of the Eucharist into the real body and blood of Christ. Without the intercession of the church and the priest, the individual had no direct contact with God. In the performance of the sacraments, it was the priest alone who could bring God into direct touch with the laity. It was this mediating role which made the church such a powerful institution.

In practice, the most enthusiastic public interest in religious observance revolved around what one historian has called a passionate 'appetite for the divine'. The 'miracles' of the sacraments were often interpreted as magical acts, and led to the adoption of a range of popular practices, from the fervent worship of relics, saints, and images to the superstitious use (through theft) of holy water, the Eucharist, and holy oil. Although such magical practices went against religious orthodoxy, the church often turned a blind eye to such transgressions, eager to sustain the mystical power of the church and its authority.

However, for most people, the church provided a ritual method of living day to day, rather than a set of rigid theological beliefs. The sacraments of baptism, confirmation, marriage, and extreme unction provided rites of passage through crucial moments in an individual's life. As a consequence, many people only went to church once or twice a year, and church records reveal remarkably low attendances, as well as profound ignorance on basic points of religion. One English preacher told the story of a shepherd who when asked about the Father, Son, and Holy Ghost replied, 'The father and the son I know well for I tend their sheep, but I know not the third fellow; there is none of that name in our village.' At best, this attitude represented religious ignorance and indifference; at worst, it suggested heresy and unbelief, which took various forms throughout the Renaissance period and beyond.

In the 1440s the Bishop of Tournai, Jean Chevrot, was so concerned at the poor attendance and observation of the sacraments that he commissioned Roger van der Weyden to paint an altarpiece that would educate people in the ritual significance of the sacraments, simply entitled the *Seven Sacraments* (Fig. 13). The left panel of van der Weyden's triptych shows baptism, confirmation, and confession, while the right panel shows ordination, marriage, and extreme unction. The central panel is

13.
Roger van der Weyden's altarpiece the *Seven Sacraments* is a religious advertisement, an attempt to educate its mid-15th-century congregation in the mysteries of the sacraments.

reserved for the most important sacrament, the Eucharist, which takes place behind the revelation of Christ. To avoid any confusion, angels helpfully float above each sacrament, holding banners with explanatory verses. By using contemporary figures, architecture, and clothing, van der Weyden's triptych employs a typically Renaissance technique of 'vulgarization', where the mysteries of the church are set against modern settings that encourage the congregation's close identification with the painted image. The quiet intensity of the scene is also noticeably devoid of the jostling, hawking, joking, spitting, swearing, knitting, begging, sleeping, and even firing guns that were a daily feature of church life.

Building the Reformation

When Pope Martin V ended the factional schism and returned to Rome in 1420, 'he found it so dilapidated and deserted that it hardly bore any resemblance to a city', never mind the capital of both the former Roman Empire and the future Catholic Empire. The response of Martin and his successors was to begin an ambitious building programme that would celebrate the glory of the newly centralized Roman Church. It would also turn the city into a building site for the following 150 years. In the words of Pope Nicholas V, the laity would find their 'belief continually confirmed and daily corroborated by great buildings' that were 'seemingly made by the hand of God'. Alberti, Fra Angelico, Bramante, Michelangelo, Raphael, and Botticelli were just some of the artists who came to be associated with the rebuilding of the city over the following decades.

The biggest problem that successive popes faced was the

renovation of the crumbling basilica of St Peter's, built on the saint's tomb by Constantine in the mid-4th century. Rome was already competing with Constantinople as imperial capital of the Christian world. The competition became even fiercer once the city fell to the Ottoman Sultan Mehmed II in 1453. Not only had Mehmed taken Constantine's imperial capital, renaming it and embarking on an ambitious campaign of rebuilding; he had also converted Hagia Sophia, one of the greatest churches in Christendom, into a mosque. Rome and its popes did not want to be outshone by Istanbul and its sultans. In April 1506 Pope Julius II laid the cornerstone for the new St Peter's, having appointed Donato Bramante as its architect. The foundation medal cast by Caradosso (Fig. 14) shows how closely Bramante's original design was modelled on Hagia Sophia. Subsequent revisions by Raphael, Sangallo, and Michelangelo throughout the 16th century led to the completion of St Peter's as it looks today.

Ironically it was the cost of completing this monumental celebration of papal authority that started a protest that would ultimately challenge the core of the Catholic Church, and transform the social and political landscape of Europe forever. In 1510, four years after work began on St Peter's, and as Michelangelo laboured on his frescoes for the ceiling of the Sistine Chapel, the German monk Martin Luther arrived in Rome. His disillusionment with the corruption and conspicuous consumption he witnessed provided the inspiration for the beginning of his attack upon the abuses of the Catholic Church—the circulation of his 95 theses against indulgences in October 1517. In March of that year, the Pope had issued an indulgence to finance the building of St Peter's. An indulgence was a papal document that granted the buyer remission from the need to do penance for his sins. So

eager was the church to finance the rebuilding of Rome that indulgences were even sold to individuals to cover uncommitted future sins. The church had created a trade in salvation that allowed the individual to buy and sell deliverance. Luther was outraged. He wrote to the Archbishop of Mainz, complaining:

> Papal indulgences for the building of St Peter's are circulating under your most distinguished name ... I grieve over the wholly false impressions which the people have conceived from them; to wit—the

unhappy souls believe that if they have purchased letters of indulgence they are sure of their salvation.

Luther repeated his protest in the 95 theses famously circulated throughout the town of Wittenberg. 'Why does not the pope', wrote Luther, 'whose wealth is to-day greater than the riches of the richest, build just this one church of St Peter with his own money, rather than with the money of poor believers?' The first shot in the history of the European Reformation had been fired.

Faith wars

Like the term 'Renaissance', 'Reformation' is a retrospective term applied to the consequences of Luther's ideas. Luther did indeed set out with the idea of reforming the church, but reformation quickly turned into revolution. Luther's protest against indulgences soon crystallized into a systematic rejection of every religious assumption upon which the Catholic Church rested. Luther devastatingly argued that the individual possessed a direct relationship with God, and could not rely on the mediation of priests, saints, or indulgences to grant salvation; the individual could only maintain absolute faith in the grace of an inscrutable but ultimately merciful God in the hope of being saved. Luther's early teachings drew on the texts of St Paul: 'For by grace are ye saved through faith; and that not of yourselves: it is the gift of God: not of works' (Ephesians 2:8–9). There was nothing that the inherently weak and evil individual could do in the face of God, but hold on to faith, the ultimate gift from God. Worldly attempts to change the state of one's soul through indulgences and penances were meaningless. As Luther himself concluded, 'A

Christian has all that he needs in faith and needs no works to justify him'.

The implication of all this for the Catholic Church was profound. Having rejected papal mediation between God and the individual, at a stroke Luther rejected the authority of both pope and priest. The theatre and paraphernalia of church ritual were rejected, as was the distinction between clergy and laity. Luther also condemned all but two of the sacraments. He argued that God gave faith directly to the individual, and did not appear through intermediaries, be they priests or sacramental rituals. The impact of Luther's ideas was complex but immediate. As he refined and expanded his position in response to increasingly alarmed Catholic responses, 'Lutheranism' spread throughout northern Europe with astonishing speed and profound consequences way beyond Luther's control. By the time of his death in 1546, councils with reformed church tendencies controlled Wittenberg, Nuremberg, Strasbourg, Zurich, Berne, and Basle. Lutheranism found fertile ground amongst a predominantly civic, urban laity disaffected with Catholicism. Monastic orders and traditional worship were abolished, church property was smashed or confiscated, and religious images were destroyed in iconoclastic riots. In their place came new sites and methods of worship, and idealistic experiments in social and political reform. In 1524 the German peasants rose up, seeking justification for their grievances in Luther's teachings. He contemptuously condemned the 'poisonous, hurtful' rebellion, revealing the limits of his radicalism when it came to more worldly matters.

Luther was also unable to control the intellectual impact of many of his arguments. In Zurich Huldreich Zwingli developed an even sparser form of Lutheranism, arguing that the Eucharist was a symbolic, not literal, communion with God. By the 1540s Geneva was under the control of the austere theology of John Calvin, who argued that man was powerless to influence divine predestination. For Calvin, God had always already decided who would be damned and who saved. Even more extreme sects inspired by Lutheranism flourished, such as Anabaptism. In England, Henry VIII's political decision to split from Rome in 1533 opened the way for Lutheranism to take hold there. In 1570 the Pope excommunicated Henry's daughter, Queen Elizabeth I, for what was by then called her 'Protestantism'. Lutheranism was here to stay.

Printing the Word

Humanism and printing lay at the heart of the rise and spread of Luther's ideas. Luther, his successor Philipp Melanchthon, Zwingli, and Calvin all utilized humanist training in philology, rhetoric, and translation to produce a theology based on 'the Word' and 'Scripture alone'. What united reformers like Luther and humanists including Erasmus was a commitment to close biblical interpretation, or exegesis, that challenged the perceived ignorance and superstition of earlier scholastic thinking. Luther could match the finest papal scholarship, boasting in his discussion *On Translating* (1530) that, 'I can do their dialectics and philosophy better than all of them put together'. But he parted company with humanism when he realized the limits of its commitment to change, writing to Erasmus in 1525, 'it matters little to you what anyone believes anywhere, as long as the peace of the world is undisturbed'. However, humanism had already supplied Luther and his followers with the intellectual tools to transform religion. It had also provided Luther with the object that would transmit his new ideas all over Europe: the printing press.

Writing on the spread of his ideas in 1522, Luther claimed 'I did nothing; the Word did everything'. He was right. It was the medium of print that so effectively circulated 'the Word'. Earlier challengers to papal authority had little ability to circulate their ideas to a wider audience, but the technology of the printing press allowed Luther to disseminate his ideas in thousands of printed books, broadsides, and pamphlets. The German states were also the perfect location from which to spread a religious revolution, being at the geographical and technological heart of Europe. By 1520 62 German cities possessed printing presses, and between 1517 and 1524 the publication of printed books in these cities increased sevenfold. One of the reasons for this increased output was Luther himself. He soon realized the radical potential of the printing press, calling it 'God's highest and extremest act of grace, whereby the business of the Gospel is driven forward'. Between 1517 and 1520 Luther wrote over 30 tracts, with more than 300,000 copies printed. One admiring friend claimed that, 'Luther is the man who can keep two printers busy, each working two presses'. Luther also realized the power of spreading his Word in the vernacular, rather than the elite church language of Latin. In 1534 Luther's German translation of the Bible was printed in Wittenberg. By 1575 it had sold an estimated 100,000 copies. It has been further estimated that his works represented one third of all German-language books sold between 1518 and 1525. By 1530, Luther had become the first best-selling author in the short history of print.

For those who could not read Luther's books, sympathetic artists like Albrecht Dürer and Lucas Cranach produced simple, cheap woodcut illustrations that visually transmitted his ideas. Cranach's woodcut known as *Passional Christi und Antichristi* (Fig. 15) is an illustration for Philipp Melanchthon's 1521 prayer book. Melanchthon added a commentary to Cranach's two woodcuts, but no words were needed to understand the message. On the left, Christ drives the moneylenders from the church, but on the right his place has been taken by the Antichrist, clearly identified as the pope, presiding over the sale of indulgences. Combining art and mass education, Lutheran artists also carefully redefined their own social role, now that the creation of statuary, frescoes, and altarpieces was condemned as 'idolatrous'. The alliance between Luther and the printing press ensured that neither religion nor art would ever be the same again.

15.
Lucas Cranach was a keen supporter of the Protestant Reformation, and these woodcuts of the Pope as Antichrist designed in 1521 were mass-produced, highly effective religious propaganda.

A can of worms

Lutheranism emerged from a world in which the commercial, financial, and political centre of gravity had gradually shifted northwards. By the beginning of the 16th century Antwerp was overtaking Venice as the commercial capital of Europe, and the German states that gave birth to Lutheranism were also forging new political identities that would create a recognizably modern map of Europe by the end of the century.

In June 1519 Charles V of the House of Hapsburg added Austria to his dynastic inheritance of Spain, Naples, the Netherlands, and the New World. This made him an ideal candidate for the vacant title of Holy Roman Emperor, which since Roman times had gradually eroded in importance, and now involved possession of scattered territories throughout Germany, Italy, and Central Europe. Although the title had become increasingly moribund, Charles saw the opportunity to use it as a platform from which to take control of western Europe. He secured the crown after bribing the German state rulers thanks to massive loans from the Augsburg financier Jakob Fugger. However, this was only the start of Charles's problems. His election alienated his rivals for the title Henry VIII and Francis I and threatened the power of the papacy itself. It initiated a monumental political power-struggle throughout Europe that saw Charles, Francis, and Henry, as well as John III of Portugal and Sultan Süleyman, vie for territorial and political control, with the city states of Italy reduced to the status of helpless bargaining counters. The seeds of nationalist revolt were also beginning to stir in northern Europe, and to the east Charles faced the overwhelming imperial power of Süleyman, who conquered Belgrade in 1521 and by 1529 was laying siege to Vienna. The rise of Lutheranism only compounded Charles's difficulties.

In 1521 Charles convened the Imperial Diet at Worms as part of his construction of a workable imperial administration. Also on the agenda was Luther's recent papal excommunication. At first Charles was keen not to alienate his German allies by excommunicating one of its monks on papal orders. However, following Luther's personal promise to the emperor himself that 'I cannot and I will not retract anything, since it is neither safe nor right to go against conscience', Charles condemned him as 'a notorious heretic'. However, Charles's sentence at Worms did not secure Luther's doom. The German states resisted papal calls for the destruction of 'Protestantism', as it was called from 1529 when a group of German princes 'protested' against calls for the condemnation of Lutheranism. Charles was repeatedly distracted by the administration of his overseas possessions as well as being faced with the spectre of Sultan Süleyman the Magnificent beating at the door of his own empire.

By 1529 Süleyman's empire stretched across North Africa, the Mediterranean, and most of eastern Europe, and was in league with Charles's enemy, Francis I. Francis marvelled at Süleyman's imperial ambitions, reporting that 'he detests the emperor [Charles V] and his title of *Caesar*, he, the Turk, causing himself to be called *Caesar*'. While the Ottomans continued to confront Charles as political equals, their faith also became an issue in the increasingly polarized religious atmosphere of the 1520s. Like Francis, Luther and his followers considered the possibility of a strategic alliance with the Ottomans as a bulwark against the religious intolerance of Charles's Hapsburg Empire. As Süleyman laid siege to Vienna, the Protestant Philip of Hesse wrote to Luther, suggesting 'not to render any aid' to Charles and his brother Ferdinand of Austria 'unless his Majesty were first to promise that we would be left in peace and not disturbed because of the Gospel'. Luther carefully studied the Koran, and participated in the publication of several German texts on Islam. Following the calls of various Lutheran pamphleteers to 'seek the enemy in Italy, not in the East!' he cautiously argued that 'if we must have any Turkish war, we ought to begin with ourselves'. This cleverly suggested that the Turkish threat was sent by God to plague the Catholic emperor and pope. Süleyman also realized how Lutheranism could play into Ottoman hands by distracting the Hapsburgs from concentrating on the military threat from the east. He is reported to have discussed the possibility of extending his imperial patronage to Luther with several European embassies. He also encouraged prayers in the mosques of Istanbul celebrating the rise of Lutheranism and the divisions of the Hapsburgs. Both Islam and Protestantism were aware that theologically their belief in the power of the book and opposition to idolatry made a political rapprochement a distinct possibility in the volatile years of the mid-16th century.

Charles V was far less ideologically flexible. His dynastic heritage was firmly based on the intolerant expulsion of both the Jews and the Moors from Spain in 1492. He and his advisers soon became convinced that Luther and Süleyman represented two sides of the same coin, both 'heretics' that must be exterminated. In 1523 the papal nuncio based in Nuremberg wrote that, 'we are occupied with the negotiations for the general war against the Turk, and for that particular war against that nefarious Martin Luther, who is a greater evil to Christendom than the Turk'. In 1530 Cardinal Campeggio wrote to Charles that Luther's

PLATE 1: Hans Holbein's *The Ambassadors*, an icon of the Renaissance, yet only rediscovered in the 19th century. Its enigmatic sitters and objects offer a wealth of insights into the period

PLATE 2: Gentile Bellini's portrait of Mehmed the Conqueror (c.1479), a western portrait commissioned by an Islamic ruler that emphasizes the vigorous exchange of art and politics between east and west

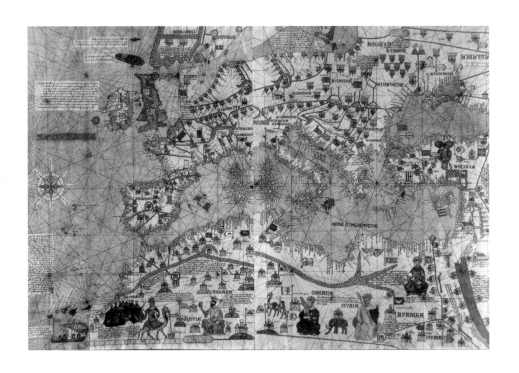

PLATE 3. The Jewish mapmaker Abraham Cresques's depiction of the riches of North Africa and its rulers, from his enormous world map made for Charles V of France in 1375

PLATE 4. This opulent printed edition of Aristotle's *Works* simulates the appearance of a manuscript with its painted jewels and hand-painted landscapes. Aristotle's disputation with Averroës emphasizes ongoing exchanges between east and west

PLATE 5. The fresco the *Donation of Constantine* was painted in the Vatican by Raphael's workshop between 1523 and 1524. Religious conflict shapes its imperial content and mannered, aggressive style

PLATE 6. Fra Angelico's *Linaiuoli Altarpiece*, completed in 1433, was created by diverse hands and intended for a variety of functions. The doors could be opened or closed to create different effects

PLATE 7. Costanzo da Ferrara's exquisite *Seated Scribe*, painted during a trip to the east between 1470 and 1480 reveals the artist's admiration of the style of Ottoman and Persian portraiture

PLATE 8. The Persian master Bihzăd's *Portrait of a Painter*. Here a Persian artist directly responds to an Italian work – Costanzo da Ferrara's *Seated Scribe* – which itself borrows from Islamic art

'diabolical and heretical opinions . . . shall be castigated and punished according to the rule and practice observed in Spain with regard to the Moors'.

This conflation of Turk and Protestant is most vividly captured in one of the most famous of all Renaissance paintings of imperial power, Titian's *Charles V at the Battle of Mühlberg* (Fig. 16), painted in 1548. The painting celebrates Charles's victory over the Lutheran forces led by Philip of Hesse at Mühlberg a year earlier, but it also echoes his earlier victory over Turkish forces at Tunis in 1535. Charles's horse is recognizable as an 'Andalusian' breed, a cross of Spanish and Arabic blood: he masters the 'infidel' horse in the same way that he hoped to crush Protestant 'heresy'. Titian rejected advice to place trampled Protestants under the horse's hooves, although in comparable equestrian images that celebrated Charles's victory at Tunis, Turks were indeed shown under the hoof. Audiences were clearly invited to read this more sinister message into the painting. One of the consequences of the Reformation was to polarize the ideological and religious differences between east and west, as both the Roman Church and the Hapsburg Empire adopted an increasingly defensive and militarily aggressive stance against Protestants, Jews, and Muslims.

As the zeal for religious reformation collided with increasingly ambitious claims to global political authority, religious intolerance intensified. Jewish communities had lived throughout Europe for centuries, in spite of their official expulsion from England in 1290 and Spain in 1492. However, in such a period of polarized religious positions, the Jews soon found themselves persecuted and used as scapegoats by both Catholics and Protestants, accused of crimes that ranged from poisoning wells to

16.
Titian's portrait of Charles V (1548) celebrates victory over the Protestants at Mühlberg in 1547, but the dark Andalusian horse also evokes Charles's battle against another group of 'unbelievers', the Ottoman Turks.

murdering Christian babies. In 1555 Pope Paul IV issued a papal bull attacking the Jewish faith, claiming that the church only 'tolerates Jews in order that they may bear witness to true Christian faith'. Jews could convert to Catholicism, otherwise they were forbidden to own property, and were confined to ghettoes where they were required to wear a yellow badge as a sign of infamy. Protestantism was hardly any more tolerant. In 1514 Luther claimed that 'the Jews will always curse and blaspheme God and his King Christ'. Many years later he claimed 'I would rather have the Turks for enemies than the Spaniards for protectors: for barbarous tyrants as they are, most of the Spaniards are half Moors, half Jews, fellows who believe nothing at all'. The Spanish Catholics in turn saw Protestants as heretics also comparable to Turks and Jews. As Catholicism responded to the threat of Lutheranism, and Protestantism tried to define itself in clear theological distinction to other religions, both increasingly attacked the two religions of the book that did not subscribe to the belief that Jesus was the Son of God.

However, Charles V had little moral right to justify his title as Defender of the Catholic Faith and leader of a holy war against all unbelievers. In 1526 Pope Clement VII attempted to oppose the Hapsburg domination of Europe. In 1527, to bring the papacy back into line, Charles allowed his imperial army (including Lutheran mercenaries) to sack Rome itself. Nearly half of the population of 55,000 were slaughtered. The papacy had finally been eclipsed as a political force, at a terrible cost.

As the papacy in Rome sensed its political power being eroded, it responded with even more lavish displays of art and architecture in an attempt to reaffirm its authority. The strain showed in the art of Michelangelo and Raphael, often seen as the ultimate manifestations of 'High Renaissance' art, and two of the greatest of all the artists commissioned to refashion Rome. Michelangelo's frescoes of scenes from Genesis that decorate the Sistine Chapel, commissioned by Pope Julius II, offer a comprehensive view of creation based on the teachings of Rome. The graceful dynamism of the scenes and the powerful, straining musculature of its characters also idealize the power and potential wrath of the Roman Church if questioned. This tension is also detectable in Raphael's frescoes for the Vatican's Salon of Constantine, commissioned by Pope Leo X in 1519. Begun by Raphael and his workshop just before the artist's death in 1520, these four huge frescoes tell the story of the life of the Emperor Constantine, each flanked by eight over-lifesize portraits of famous popes. The Salon and its decoration proclaimed the imperial authority of the papacy, and the shift in church power from the east (Constantine's imperial seat of Constantinople) to the west (St Peter's in Rome). The final scene in the fresco cycle, entitled *Donation of Constantine* (Plate 5), shows the Emperor Constantine handing over his worldly and imperial power to the pope, wearing a tiara that demonstrates both his spiritual and worldly power. The fresco boldly rejects Lutheran attacks on both the political power of the papacy and intellectual attacks on the *Donation* itself. In February 1520, just months after work began on the Constantine Salon, Luther wrote, 'I have at hand Lorenzo Valla's proof that the Donation of Constantine is a forgery. Good heavens, what darkness and wickedness is at Rome. You wonder at the judgement of God that such unauthentic, crass, impudent lies not only lived, but prevailed for so many centuries'. Valla's treatise on the *Donation* had been printed for the first time in Germany in 1517 as part of the growing attack upon the Roman Church. The frescoes in the Salon of Constantine, with their towering popes, warring factions, and dramatic scenes of papal authority are aggressive, mannered, and anxious responses to religious and political change. They represent the rise of the artistic style that would come to be labelled 'Mannerism'. The printed 'word' from the north was triumphing over the towering monuments and glorious frescoes of the south.

The empire strikes back

The Roman Church soon realized that triumphant art was no answer to the questions posed by the dramatic rise of northern European Protestantism. In March 1545 Pope Paul III finally managed to convene the Council of Trent to reform the church from within and formalize its refutation of the Lutheran Reformation. Over the next 18 years the council met intermittently to draft decrees that formed the basis of the Catholic Counter-Reformation. The Council reaffirmed the sanctity of the seven sacraments, transubstantiation, purgatory, and papal authority. It endorsed the veneration of saints, relics, and the purchase of indulgences, while also reforming the manifest abuses that had so angered Luther. Religious orders were reformed, seminaries were established for the training of priests, and bishops were expected to take a more proactive approach to the administration of their dioceses. In its more aggressive decisions the Council endorsed the creation in 1540 of the Society of Jesus (better known as the Jesuit order), led by the Spaniard Ignatius Loyola, and the establishment in 1542 of the Roman Inquisition that hunted down heretics and reformers.

The Council also turned its attention to the most pernicious carrier of the Protestant Reformation—the printed book. In 1563 it issued an index of forbidden books deemed 'heretical', declaring 'if anyone should read or possess books by heretics or writings by any author condemned and prohibited by reason of heresy or suspicion of false teaching, he incurs immediately the sentence of excommunication'. The Index forbade thousands of books, starting with the works of Luther, Zwingli, and Calvin, but also including the works of Machiavelli and selected writings of Erasmus. Other books were bowdlerized, including Boccaccio's *Decameron* and Castiglione's *The Courtier*. Trent implicitly conceded the power of the printed book (partly through the funding of Catholic printing presses to publish orthodox texts), but at the cost of establishing one of the first modern attempts at mass censorship.

The Council of Trent's zealous mix of reform, piety, militancy, and repression was remarkably successful. It has been calculated that by the end of the 16th century nearly a third of the laity lost to Rome had returned to the fold as a result of the Counter-Reformation. However, its increasingly assertive and intolerant attitude towards religious observance, books, and even images further polarized the religious landscape of the later 16th century. Trent underlined the widening gulf between the ideology of Protestantism and Catholicism, and in the process paved the way for the religious wars of the latter half of the century that would redefine the shape of Europe.

By 1600, Europe had changed beyond all recognition from the ill-defined collection of city states and principalities that made little reference to the entity of 'Europa' in 1400. Nation states and emerging global empires set the political agenda, and the fluidity of religious encounters and exchanges between east and west had hardened into the programmatic belief systems of Catholicism, Protestantism, and Islam. This signalled the birth of the modern institution of the state and the concomitant rise of nationalism. The great imperial powers of Europe would go on to claim most of the newly discovered globe over the next three centuries. But the legacy of the period was also a series of seemingly irresolvable religious and political conflicts in regions as diverse as Ireland, Mexico, and the Balkans, whose origins lay in the collision of church and state that first took place in the Renaissance.

4. Putting things into perspective

The lives of the artists

In 1550 the Tuscan artist Giorgio Vasari published a book that single-handedly invented the idea of Renaissance art. One of the classics of art history, Vasari's *Lives of the Most Excellent Painters, Sculptors and Architects* (known as the *Lives of the Artists*) consisted of 142 biographies of artists, beginning with the birth of the Florentine painter Giovanni Cimabue in 1240, and culminating in the achievements of Michelangelo in the first half of the 16th century. The *Lives* has become the bible of Renaissance art, a defining and abiding statement on the artistic 'spirit' of the period.

Vasari was the first writer to use the Italian word 'rinascita' (or 'rebirth') to describe the revolution in art that began in the late 13th century and which reached its pinnacle in the mid-16th century. Vasari argued that Cimabue and Giotto represented the first age that 'banished completely that rude Greek manner and revived the modern and good art of painting, introducing the portraying well from nature of living people'. Architecture also reacted against what Vasari saw as the 'barbarous' 'manner of buildings that are called by us to-day German'. What he dismissively called 'Greek' and 'German' would today be categorized as Byzantine and Gothic art. Vasari's second age represented an 'infinite improvement in everything' produced in the first age, and was exemplified by the 15th-century Florentine architect Filippo Brunelleschi, who 'recovered the measures and proportions of the ancients', and insisted that 'all works should proceed by rule, should be pursued with better ordering, and should be distributed with due measure'. For Vasari, the second age represented the triumph of technical form, measurement, proportion, and above all perspective. However, the culmination of this mastery came with the third age, represented by Leonardo, Raphael, and, above all others, the 'divine' Michelangelo. Their mastery of colour, perspective, and proportion 'surpassed the age of the ancients', and convinced Vasari 'that art has done everything that it is possible for her, as an imitator of nature, to do'.

Vasari's account was a brilliant public relations exercise that validated the status of the artist as a professional. Before the publication of the *Lives*, art was seen as a dirty, dubious workmanlike activity. Vasari saw the opportunity to elevate his craft to the level of divinity. Writing at the end of the Renaissance, he was perfectly placed to define the artistic transformation of the period on his own terms. However, Vasari's account was highly selective, exclusively Italian, and predominantly Florentine. He confined the northern European art of van Eyck and Dürer to just seven pages. His story was also suspiciously free of the upheavals in politics, religion, and commerce within the period. One way of showing how selective Vasari's account of Renaissance art really was is to look at his own artistic career, to see if he practised what he preached in his *Lives*.

Vasari was one of the most successful painters in 16th-century Italy, building his career upon an astute ability to give his powerful patrons what they wanted. He worked extensively for both the papacy in Rome and the Medici in Florence. In 1572 he returned to Rome, having secured a commission from Pope Gregory XIII to decorate the Vatican's Sala Regia. The Hall was designed to celebrate Catholic authority which was experiencing severe criticism and hostility. Vasari's response was to create a series of frescoes that showed the militant, aggressive side of the Catholic Church. Vasari's 1573 fresco *The Massacre of Coligny and the Huguenots on St Bartholomew's Day, 24 August 1572* (Fig. 17) celebrated the infamous slaughter of thousands of French Protestants by Catholics in Paris just months earlier. Days before the massacre Pope Gregory was reported to have said that 'for the exaltation of the Catholic faith, we desire nothing else than the extermination of the Huguenots'. Vasari vividly depicts the Huguenot leader Admiral Coligny being thrown out of an upstairs window, while his followers (shown as deformed demons) are put to the sword in the foreground. Alongside his depiction of the massacre in Paris, Vasari painted frescoes of the Catholic Alliance's destruction of the Turkish naval fleet at the Battle of Lepanto in 1571.

These beautiful but violent frescoes show Vasari enthusiastically endorsing the Catholic Church's belligerent attempt to eliminate all forms of religious 'unbelief', be it Protestantism or Islam. They also show how Renaissance art was commissioned in the service of religion and politics, a dimension rarely discussed by Vasari in his writings. This is hardly surprising, as the third and greatest age of art, represented by Michelangelo, Raphael, Titian, and Vasari himself, was also the age in which the Catholic Church employed art in its uncompromising and highly political counter-attack against the Protestant Reformation. As a result, there is little space in Vasari for northern, Protestant art, or the equally 'ungodly' art of the east and its fertile interactions with the more orthodox art of 15th-century Italy. Vasari's approach to Renaissance art, persuasive as it is, should be treated with some caution. Other approaches need to be considered to

17.
Vasari's fresco *The Massacre of Coligny and the Huguenots on St Bartholomew's Day* (1572) revels in violence and religious conflict, topics not addressed in his *Lives of the Artists*.

supplement the idealized portrait that Vasari paints for the reader of the *Lives*.

Vasari's account of Renaissance art is, however, useful because it is written from the perspective of a successful practising artist. For Vasari, the stylistic and formal development of art is of primary importance. The social function and reception of art, and the related issues of politics, patronage, religion, and history, are merely secondary to aesthetic considerations. Vasari is also often reluctant to admit the importance of patronage because one of his aims is to exalt the role of the artist as the prime creative force in any composition, and not the patron. In fact, the Renaissance witnessed radical changes in relations between artist and patron, as well as transformations in art's relation to trade, politics, and religion.

Different perspectives on Renaissance art

Religious instruction formed much of the early impetus for the creation of Renaissance art. In his late 13th-century manuscript the *Catholicon*, the Italian grammarian John of Genoa argued:

> ... there were three reasons for the institutions of images in churches. *First*, for the instruction of simple people, because they are instructed by them as if by books. *Second*, so that the mystery of the incarnation and the examples of the Saints may be the more active in our memory through being presented daily to our eyes. *Third*, to excite feelings of devotion, these being aroused more effectively by things seen than by things heard.

Visual images of religious themes could educate and instruct a congregation, as well as intensify emotion and faith. Images, or icons, were often imbued with magical, devotional, and didactic functions, from intensifying identification with the Virgin Mary to providing a defence against the plague or bad weather. Built into the design of churches thanks to the patronage of wealthy citizens, images were often used as the focus of public religious rituals or private devotional reflection.

While the church saw the importance of art as a method of instruction, it also faced a biblical injunction against images. The Old Testament forbade the making of 'any graven image, nor the likeness of anything that is in heaven above nor in the earth below' (Exodus 20: 4). Theologians like St Thomas Aquinas worried that such images would simply be worshipped for their earthly beauty, rather than as a means of coming closer to God. 'Religion', argued Aquinas, 'does not offer worship to images considered as mere things in themselves, but as images drawing us to God incarnate. Motion to an image does not stop there at the image but goes on to the thing it represents.' Worship of the image itself was idolatry; the aim was to see the art object as something that enabled the viewer to come closer to God. Many 15th-century clerics worried that lavishly designed images created a reverence for 'gold and jewels, and not the figures, or rather, the truths represented by those figures'. This friction between the sacred ideals and profane possibilities of images ran throughout all of Renaissance art, suggesting that religious hopes and worldly expectations were inextricably entwined.

Another significant aspect of early Renaissance art is that works were frequently a collaborative effort produced by diverse hands, with little distinction made between the 'artist' and other skilled craftsmen. Artists invariably doubled as gold- or silversmiths, bronze casters, stonecutters and carvers, carpenters, plasterers, and wood-carvers, as well as painters and sculptors.

The utilization of a particular skill was based on the nature of the object an artist was commissioned to produce. Images, be they painted, illuminated, carved, cast, stained, woven, or embroidered adorned objects as diverse as bedsteads, musical instruments, horse trappings, armour, and wedding chests, not to mention altarpieces, chapels, and tombs. As this list suggests, commissions often specified the use of precious materials over and above creative skill and innovation. Gold, silver, bronze, marble, hardwood, glass, wool, coral, diamonds, and pearls were just some of the many expensive materials that a patron could insist on building into any commission.

To deal with the cost and diverse expertise involved in successfully undertaking such commissions, virtually every artist was attached to a workshop. The workshop made and sold objects, pooled resources and expertise, and passed on its skills from masters to apprentices. By 1478 Florence's population of around 60,000 contained 54 sculptors' shops, 44 goldsmiths' shops, and 40 painters' shops. Most painters, sculptors, and masons were also attached to a guild or corporation that regulated standards, mediated relations between patrons, masters, and apprentices, financially supported its members, and organized festivals, services, and processions. The workshop and the guild promoted collaboration, competition, and cross-fertilization of styles and techniques.

An exploration of the significance of what appears to be a quintessentially religious image from the early period of the Renaissance provides a graphic example of the different ways in which art was commissioned, produced, and received in the early 15th century. The Dominican Fra Angelico's *Linaiuoli Altarpiece* (Plate 6) was commissioned by the Florentine wool cloth merchants (or *linaiuoli*) in 1432 and installed in their offices in Florence in 1433. Our modern eye is immediately drawn to Fra Angelico's exquisite panel painting of the Madonna and Child surrounded by angels. On its outer doors Fra Angelico painted St Peter and St Paul, with scenes of their lives (including the martyrdom of St Mark in Alexandria) and the Adoration of the Magi on the base, or predella. When opened the doors of the altarpiece revealed St John the Baptist (on the left) and St John the Evangelist (on the right).

The friar was just one of several skilled craftsmen commissioned to create the altarpiece. Another artist, Lorenzo Ghiberti, predominantly celebrated for his sculpture, designed the marble frame. Two Florentine stonecutters carved it, while another artist made the wooden base and doors. The close collaboration and exchange between this collection of artists is reflected in Fra Angelico's use of perspective and foreshortening in the predella scenes, an experimental technique being developed at the time by Ghiberti and his Florentine colleagues Masaccio and Brunelleschi. It is a modern conceit to ascribe the altarpiece to its primary painter, in this case Fra Angelico; he was just one of the many diverse hands that made the complete object. The contract for the altarpiece also stipulated that its design, cost, and appearance were in the hands of the commissioning guild, not the artist. The potentially idolatrous nature of 15th-century religious art meant that, in the memorable words of Michael Baxandall, 'painting was still too important to be left to the painters'. The artists were to stick closely to the agreed drawing, and the religious friar was to receive a very worldly payment of 'one hundred and ninety gold florins' for his labour.

The cloth merchants were also aware of the secular and worldly impact of commissioning a sumptuous altarpiece. By ordering such an object, the guild expressed its religious piety, but also celebrated its secular wealth and commercial authority to the wider community in its ability to command the skills of such craftsmen, and afford their expensive materials. Their own commercial trade was given legitimacy and prestige in the small portrayal of the Adoration of the Magi at the foot of the altarpiece, where a young man kneels bearing the gift of a bolt of dyed crimson cloth for the infant Jesus. The religious aura of the painting is thus shot through with commercial interests. The contract also indicates that during the day the doors were to be opened to reflect the golden aura of the Madonna, child, and St Johns. At night the more sombre images of the two St Pauls were to be displayed, which suggests that the altarpiece had very different devotional uses at different times. As this alterpiece shows, to fully appreciate a Renaissance art object it is necessary to understand the original context of the commission, the significance of its location, and the various social, political, and religious functions that it served.

Our friends in the north

As Fra Angelico's altarpiece reveals, skilled collaboration, deferral to the requirements of the patron, concern with precious materials, specific setting and context, and productive tensions between religious and secular worlds were all hallmarks of early Renaissance art. Though Vasari had little to say about the artistic significance of Jan van Eyck and his contemporaries Roger van der Weyden and Jean Fouquet, art in northern Europe was also flourishing at this time, and indeed it was here that the technique of oil painting was perfected. Just as Fra Angelico was completing his *Linaiuoli Altarpiece* in Florence, van Eyck began work on one of the most iconic of all Renaissance images, the *Arnolfini Double Portrait* (Fig. 18).

Completed in 1434, van Eyck's painting is very different to Fra Angelico's altarpiece. Its remarkable visual realism, attention to domestic detail, delicately glazed use of oil paint and secular subject matter seem to be a world away from the religious intensity, collaborative workmanship, and opulent gold leaf of Fra Angelico's altarpiece. Michelangelo famously criticized Flemish painting 'because it attempts to do so many things well (each one of which would suffice for greatness) that it does none well'. This microscopic attention to detail is the first thing that strikes the viewer of van Eyck's painting, although Michelangelo's criticism smacks more of Italian cultural nationalism than objective art criticism. Northern European art emerged from significantly different traditions from those that informed the creation of Italian art. Patronage, guild structures, political authority, and even religious observance all developed in noticeably different ways north of the Alps, and the result is reflected in van Eyck's painting. While van Eyck did not invent the technique of oil painting, he did perfect the method of using an oil-glaze. This involved layers of translucent pigment being patiently applied on top of one another, creating the brilliant glow and delicate modulation of colour seen in the *Arnolfini Double Portrait*. The bright, even light of Italy lacked the subtle climatic variation of northern Europe, a simple issue that profoundly influenced the stylistic differences in colour, light, and shade that distinguishes Fra Angelico from van Eyck. Factors such as this were often as

18.
Jan van Eyck's
Arnolfini Portrait
(1434) lavishes as
much attention on
the interior decor
and the
consumable
objects as on the
couple themselves.

important in defining the contrasting aesthetic of northern and southern European art as differences in patronage and guild structure.

Van Eyck's painting depicts a modern domestic scene that appears to celebrate the marriage of the couple in an elegantly furnished Flemish bedroom. The husband appears to be making a vow, while the woman's slightly raised dress, and the close proximity of the bed, suggests that the painting anticipates her future (or recently revealed) pregnancy. Some critics see the picture as both a 'pictorial marriage certificate' and a painted fertility symbol. Yet what also stands out is the picture's remarkable detail. The dog and clogs, the window with its light flooding in, and the elaborate brass chandelier, carved gargoyle, and convex mirror hanging on the far wall are all rendered with meticulous attention to detail.

The couple represented in the painting are Giovanni di Arrigo Arnolfini, a wealthy and politically powerful Italian merchant who worked in Bruges from 1421 until his death in 1472, and his wife Giovanna, the daughter of another Italian merchant. Arnolfini sold cloth and tapestries to van Eyck's patron, Duke Philip, and rose to be governor of finance for Normandy. While the painting acts as a pious image of Arnolfini's marriage, it also displays the wealth and luxury that comes with his commercial expertise and political power. This is an image that worships acquisition and possession, from Arnolfini's wife to the expensive Baltic furs, Spanish oranges, Venetian glasswork, Ottoman carpets, and German woodwork that van Eyck renders with such loving detail. The painting celebrates Arnolfini's position as a key player in the emerging world of international trade, vividly expressed in the precious commodities that are painted with as much precision as the Arnolfini couple. The painting's ethos is captured in a contemporary Spanish account of Bruges:

... anyone who has money and wishes to spend it will find in this town everything that the whole world produces. I saw there oranges and lemons from Castile, which seemed only just to have been gathered from the trees, fruits and wine from Greece, as abundant as in that country. I saw also confections and spices from Alexandria and all the Levant, just as if one were there; furs from the Black Sea, as if they had been produced in the district. Here was all Italy with its brocades, silks and armour and everything which is made there; and indeed there is no part of the world whose products are not found here at their best.

The emphasis on the freshness and sensuousness of these international goods all gathered in one place is reproduced in the seductive illusionism in van Eyck's painting of the texture and sheen of fruit, silk, fur, and glass.

Van Eyck's use of perspective leads our eye to the convex mirror on the back wall. His use of a mirror suggests that van Eyck was also fascinated by new developments in optics, which he used to create his incredibly vivid representations of domestic life. He was shrewdly taking advantage of the changing nature of the commercial and technological developments that he witnessed all around him. The mirror reflects the scene before us and two shadowy figures that have just entered the room. Above the mirror is the inscription 'Jan van Eyck was here / 1434'. Looking more closely at the reflection, we can see van Eyck himself, a figure in blue, acting more like a priest at a wedding than an artist painting a portrait. The painter daringly places himself right at the centre of his own composition, asserting his role as creator, mischievously comparing his status to that of a priest. The same tension between the religious and the secular identified in Fra Angelico's altarpiece is evident here, as van Eyck boldly asserts the artist's importance as equivalent to both patron's and sitter's. It is the artist who claims to know best, a belief that anticipates the ways in which artists from Michelangelo to Picasso would increasingly assert personal autonomy in the creation of their art.

Back to the east

Renaissance art and its social and religious importance developed in noticeably distinct ways in the north and south, but it also circulated between east and west. Fra Angelico's portrayal of the martyrdom of St Mark in Alexandria, and van Eyck's sensual depiction of precious objects and materials of the east emphasize the ways in which artistic creativity of the period drew much of its inspiration from the wealth and commodities of the east. Just three years before completing his *Linaiuoli Altarpiece* Fra Angelico had completed a *Madonna and Child* in the Florentine church of San Marco, complete with Arabic inscriptions on the Madonna's dress drawn from Islamic textiles and pottery, a tradition established by Giotto and Cimabue and developed by Uccello, Masaccio, and Botticelli. However, as well as objects, aesthetic styles were also exchanged between east and west. Between 1470 and 1480 the Italian artist Costanzo da Ferrara visited Istanbul and produced a series of beautiful paintings and drawings that took their inspiration from the artistic conventions of Persian and Ottoman art. His pen and gouache drawing *Seated Scribe* (Plate 7) is an intimate study of an Ottoman scribe, complete with Arabic inscription in the top right-hand corner. The attention to detail, from the scribe's opulent dress to his golden earring, reveals Costanzo's absorption of Islamic principles of figural representation. This was a process of assimilation that filtered back into grander commissioned paintings of the late 15th century that incorporated 'Oriental' figures into their scenes, of which Bellini's *Saint Mark Preaching in Alexandria* (Fig. 3) is just one of many examples. Some indication of the artistic exchange of styles and influences can be seen in a remarkable copy of Costanzo's drawing by the 15th-century Persian artist Bihzād, entitled *Portrait of a Painter in Turkish Costume* (Plate 8), executed some years after Costanzo's drawing. Bihzād learns from his Italian contemporary, while subtly changing the scribe into a painter, shown working on precisely the kind of Islamic portrait originally copied by Costanzo. Each artist draws on the aesthetic innovations of the other, making it impossible to say which painting is definably 'western' or 'eastern'. Like the learning, science, and commercial transactions with the east, this artistic exchange reflects an admiration for the skill of Islamic art, a factor crucial to the shaping of an artistic tradition that now we call 'Renaissance'. To ignore such exchanges is to only tell one side of the story of the Renaissance.

Power on display

Early 15th-century Renaissance art emerged as a result of the enhanced buying power of a predominantly urban and commercial elite keen to display their wealth through the commissioning of lavish art objects, and the eagerness of a church to manufacture and distribute a coherent theological position to the faithful. By 1453, with the fall of Constantinople, these religious and commercial developments had become evermore politicized, as the city states of western Europe confronted both internal dissent and the growing imperial power of the Ottoman Empire to the east. Art was utilized to articulate these political tensions. Art objects became increasingly monumental and public. They looked backwards to a classical past rather than biblical precedent to provide new political ideologies with intellectual credibility and authority.

Sculpture was a particularly appropriate medium for conveying claims to political authority and dominion, and one of its finest practitioners was the Florentine sculptor and stonemason Donatello. He realized that the changing nature of 15th-century politics and patronage required classical stories of public achievement and imperial aspiration as much as biblical examples of spiritual contemplation and worldly mortification. For the growing class of *condottiere*, mercenaries and military rulers of the city states of Italy, classical comparisons with imperial figures like Alexander the Great or Julius Caesar seemed far more appropriate than anything the Bible could offer. To ensure that they could continue to create expensive, innovative art works, artists like Donatello pursued classically inspired commissions from wealthy, powerful patrons that were politically sensitive but also extremely lucrative.

In 1445 Donatello moved to Padua to work on an equestrian statue of one of Venice's most successful mercenaries, the Paduan Erasmo de' Narni, nicknamed Gattamelata, or 'honeycat' (Fig. 19). This was an ambitious and difficult commission. It drew on ancient classical equestrian monuments still visible in Rome, but also required immense skill in design and casting. The statue was finally completed in 1453, with Donatello paid the enormous sum of 1,650 ducats, and erected in the town square. Everyone was happy. Donatello increased his stature as an innovative designer and caster, surpassing the technical

19.
Donatello's equestrian statue of the *condottiere* Erasmo de' Narni (*c.*1445–53) dominates Padua's Piazza del Santo. The equestrian statue was a monumental statement of both artistic skill and political authority.

achievements of the sculpture of antiquity. De' Narni's family secured an imposing art object that conferred classical respectability upon a mercenary and was astutely positioned to maximize Gattamelata's claims to civic respect and political authority. The financial and artistic demands made by Donatello and the classical nature of the subject matter were both relatively new developments in Renaissance art, as was the highly political orchestration and public display of the artwork. Perhaps most significantly, in carrying out such commissions involving the finest materials, the artist's stature increased, giving him the opportunity to work on evermore ambitious and innovative art objects.

Such classically inspired imperial images were not exclusive to 15th-century Italy. In 1481 Costanzo da Ferrara was commissioned to design a beautiful bronze portrait medal of Mehmed II (Fig. 20) that used a similar image of a powerful military ruler on horseback to broadcast the sultan's claims to imperial supremacy. Both Mehmed and his horse are recognizably 'real', although like Donatello's equestrian statue, they evoke a classical tradition of imperial power that would have been recognized by both Mehmed and his Italian political counterparts. This is another image that easily circulates between east and west, an art object commissioned by (or on behalf of) Mehmed that plays exactly the same game of political bravado exhibited by the statue of Gattamelata. The sultan commissions an equestrian image that celebrates his recent military exploits, placing his imperial power within the contexts of the classical exploits of Alexander the Great and Emperor Constantine. Mehmed actually had much more legitimate claim to such status, based on his possession of most of Central Asia, Greece, and the eastern Mediterranean. This also

partly explains the choice of art object. Rather than commissioning a huge, static equestrian statue, Mehmed's small, portable medal could be cast in hundreds, and distributed east and west to inspire rulers with appropriate fear and admiration.

The contrast between Donatello's monumental statue and Costanzo's exquisite medal emphasizes the growing sophistication of powerful patrons. None was more enthusiastic than Isabella d'Este. The marriage of Isabella to Francesco Gonzaga of Mantua in 1490 cemented a dynastic alliance between two of the most powerful political families in Italy, and allowed Isabella to embark on a career as an extremely discerning patron and collector. Her collection was initially limited to the smaller objects that reflected courtly wealth and extravagance such as medals, gems, vases, and cameos. However, Isabella appreciated that authority and magnificence resided in possession of monumental as well as small-scale art works. By 1498 she had created a network of agents to scour Italy for contemporary and antique works, following Isabella's instructions that 'we now want other things than cameos: rather, we are now interested in owning some figurines and heads in bronze and marble'. Isabella created her own apartment, or *studiolo*, for the appreciation of her various purchases and commissions, which at her death included over 1,000 coins and medals, 72 vases, 48 statues, 46 engraved gems, and personally commissioned paintings by Leonardo, Titian, Bellini, and Perugino. Isabella was also instrumental in the successful career of Andrea Mantegna, whose work for the Mantuan Gonzaga dynasty led to his social elevation to the status of a lord. As patronage increasingly defined the shape of Renaissance art, its elevation of the artist within society also transformed the status of art itself, and provided artists with increasing autonomy to create what they wanted.

Building the Renaissance

The economic expansion of the 15th century laid the foundations for one of the most dramatic and concrete manifestations of the Renaissance—its architecture. The centralization of the Catholic Church following the schisms of the 14th century changed how builders and patrons approached the construction and layout of churches, monasteries, and chapels. Increasingly churches were designed as overwhelming and enduring monuments that broadcast the universal power of the church. The rise of the Italian city states, fuelled by territorial consolidation and the concentration of economic wealth, also led to the construction of increasingly ambitious urban planning schemes and the reorganization of civic and domestic spaces that reflected this new wealth.

However, the great utopian architectural schemes that are often seen as defining the Renaissance should be approached with some caution. The Florentine artists and architects Filippo Brunelleschi and Leon Battista Alberti are often credited with revolutionizing architectural theory and design in a series of books and buildings completed in the first half of the 15th century. In 1413, Brunelleschi designed two panel paintings (subsequently lost) of two of the most important civic spaces in Florence, the Baptistery and the Palazzo Vecchio. The two-dimensional panels spectacularly created the illusion of three dimensions. Alberti formalized Brunelleschi's methods in his book *On Painting* (1435), where he explained how 'to draw with lines and paint with colours . . . surfaces that resemble any body that can be seen, so that at a fixed distance and from a fixed central position, they seem three-dimensional'.

In theory, this idealized and geometrically abstract redefinition of urban space encased individuals and their environment within a net of criss-crossing sightlines, which Alberti compared to the 'bars of a cage', which 'make what is called the visual pyramid'. These ideas were realized visually in a series of paintings of ideal cities and palaces, such as Piero di Cosimo's *The Building of a Palace* (Fig. 21). Cosimo's painting reproduces Brunelleschi and Alberti's principles of three-dimensionality and vanishing point perspective. It also suggests the possibility of a revolutionary, utopian transformation of urban space with wide piazzas, perfectly proportioned civic buildings, and classically inspired columns and arches.

In reality such images were flights of fantasy, comparable to the spectacular designs that contemporary architects draw up prior to the impact of financial and environmental realities that always compromise the final built product. The pragmatic transformation of urban spaces using the basic principles of geometry

21.
Piero di Cosimo's *The Building of a Palace (c.1515–20)* is an idealistic image of the construction of a Renaissance city that captures the magnificent aspirations of the time.

and surveying had been developing for centuries by the time that Brunelleschi and Alberti began selling the idea of perspective to their wealthy patrons. In many cases designers like Brunelleschi and Alberti were asked to complete or revise religious or civic building projects that had been started centuries before: it was only by the early 15th century that the political will and sufficient disposable wealth were available to realize such schemes.

Alberti's early architectural career is a good example of the gulf between the theory and practice of Renaissance architecture. He arrived at the court of the controversial mercenary and warlord of Rimini, Sigismondo Malatesta, in the early 1450s, flushed with the literary success of his study of the principles of architecture, *On the Art of Building* (1452). Alberti had been heavily influenced by the rediscovery of the Roman architect Vitruvius' classical study *On Architecture*. Vitruvius gave Alberti a detailed architectural vocabulary that spanned construction, function, and beauty of design. Alberti was particularly interested in Vitruvius' use of columns (Doric, Ionic, and Corinthian) and arches to express social status and power. For Alberti:

> The principal ornament to any city lies in the siting, layout, composition and arrangement of its roads, squares and individual works; each must be properly planned and distributed according to use, importance and convenience. For without order there can be nothing commodious, graceful and noble.

It was this founding principle that drew a figure like Sigismondo Malatesta to Alberti. Having established social and political 'order' through military force, Sigismondo required the concrete manifestation of grace and nobility to affirm his authority. Alberti, via the imperial Roman tradition of Vitruvius, seemed capable of providing all of this, and he was subsequently commissioned to redesign the old brick church of San Francesco.

Drawing on classical models, Alberti designed a building that looked more like a classical temple than a Catholic Church—hence its name, Tempio Malatestiano (Fig. 22). Alberti collaborated closely with the builder and sculptor Matteo de' Pasti in encasing the old church in a classical shell of Istrian stone, marble, and porphyry. The façade was replaced by a severe design that used Roman half-columns and arches borrowed from the triumphal arches of the Emperors Augustus and Constantine, appropriate classical analogies for an ambitious *condottiere* like Sigismondo. However, Alberti faced endless problems. He struggled to accommodate local materials and existing medieval structures with his classical models, and lacked skilled workers able to

22. Alberti's façade of the Tempio Malatestiano in Rimini was left unfinished due to lack of money in 1468, but represented the new international, classical architectural style.

put his vision into practice. As a result, the striking columns were crudely pieced together with mismatched stone that Sigismondo looted from nearby classical buildings! Even worse, Alberti's patron ran out of money, and the temple was left unfinished in 1468, frustrating Alberti's plan to add a second floor and lead-roofed dome in imitation of the Roman Pantheon.

Not everyone seemed comfortable with this new architectural style. Commenting on one of Alberti's Mantuan churches, Cardinal Francesco Gonzaga complained 'I could not tell whether he meant it to look like a church, a mosque or a synagogue'. However, the international flavour of Alberti's classical style found favour with aspiring imperial clients far beyond Italy. In 1460 the Ottoman Sultan Mehmed II wrote to Sigismondo to ask for the services of Matteo de' Pasti. Mehmed was embarking on the building of the Topkapi Saray (Fig. 23), which as one commentator observed, was 'a palace that should outshine all and be more

23.
The imposing Topkapi Saray Palace in Istanbul. Begun by Mehmed II in the early 1460s, and designed by an international team of architects. Most of the current structure dates from later centuries.

marvellous than all preceding palaces in looks, size, cost and gracefulness'. In a city like Constantinople, with its churches, synagogues, mosques, and the Grand Bazaar, de' Pasti's practical experience in the creation of a secular, imperial, and international style of architecture seemed extremely appropriate for Mehmed's new palace. When de' Pasti was arrested en route by the Venetian authorities, Mehmed also wooed other followers of Alberti, including Filarete and Michelozzo, whose contribution has been traced in the mixed Islamic, Greek, Roman, and Italian influences that characterized Mehmed's imposing palace. Filarete travelled on from Istanbul to Moscow, where he was involved in designs for the new Kremlin. His disciple Antonio Bonfini settled in Budapest where he translated Filarete's *Treatise* on architecture for the Hungarian King Matthias Corvinus. Bonfini congratulated Matthias for persuading the Hungarian nobility to 'build grand houses in proportion to their means', and for building 'a palace of almost Roman splendour'. No wonder Cardinal Gonzaga was bewildered at this new international style; its elegance and affirmation of political power was available to anyone who could afford it.

Several Italian city states could afford the new style, and were eager to compete with the architectural splendour and claims to imperial authority of Mehmed's palace. In the small principality of Urbino, from the 1440s until his death in 1482, the *condottiere* Federico da Montefeltro invested more money in building than any other Italian ruler of his time. In the late 1460s Federico hired the Dalmatian architect Luciano Laurana to expand his Palazzo Ducale, begun in 1444. Laurana's designs were aimed at emulating Mehmed's architectural achievements in his new city of Istanbul. Federico was a new type of patron of architecture and the arts. One of his admiring biographers, Vespasiano da Bisticci, claimed that he was instructed 'in the *Ethics* of Aristotle', and 'he was the first of the Signori who took up philosophy ... As to architecture it may be said that none of his age, high or low, knew it so thoroughly. We may see in the buildings he constructed, the grand style and the due measurement and proportion, especially in his palace, which has no superior amongst the buildings of the time'. Federico himself celebrated the skill of 'architecture, founded the arts of arithmetic and geometry, which are the foremost of the seven liberal arts because they depend upon exact certainty'. It was a skill that could fashion 'a beautiful residence worthy of the rank and fame of our ancestors and our own stature'. Here was an explicit statement of the deeply political nature of late 15th-century architecture. Its exactitude as a science enabled the creation of an imposing built environment that reflected the political power, military might, and purchasing power of a figure like Federico.

The creation of these newly designed environments involved a totally different approach to domestic and public life. Federico's absorption of Aristotle's *Ethics* added a further dimension to the Renaissance assimilation of the classical past. Aristotle's text offered a compelling defence of the political value of conspicuous cultural consumption and magnificence, arguing that:

> The magnificent man is like an artist; for he can see what is fitting and spend large sums tastefully ... A magnificent man spends not on himself but on public objects ... [he] will also furnish his house suitably to his wealth (for even a house is a sort of public ornament), and will spend by preference on those works that are lasting (for these are the most beautiful).

Within the walls of Federico's palace magnificence was being adapted to define social and political status and authority. The positioning of Federico's exquisitely designed *studiolo* (Fig. 24) encapsulated the ways in which 15th-century architecture constructed private and public space in line with the status and claims to authority of its inhabitants.

The *studiolo* was strategically located between Federico's public audience chamber and his private apartments. Here the duke could pursue his scholarly interests and display his Aristotelian 'magnificence' to visiting dignitaries and rivals. Tapestries, medals, gems, armour, books, and paintings: the extraordinary array of art works that Federico commissioned to exhibit his taste, wealth, and power emphasize the diversity of objects, materials, and skills that constituted 'Renaissance art'.

24.
Federico da Montefeltro's *studiolo* displays the *condottiere's* personal and political magnificence in its illusionistic inlaid wood panelling, and strikingly oriental portraits of classical philosophers.

The intricate intarsia (inlaid wood decoration) of the *studiolo* also illustrates how innovative art of the period required the purchasing power and political authority of influential patronage. The deceptive illusionism of the *studiolo* plays games with perspective and foreshortening, revealing 'open' cupboards full of books, scientific and musical instruments, political portraits, armorial devices, and panoramas of ideal cities of the type envisaged by Alberti. The message is clear. Federico's mastery of the arts, architecture, science, and military matters reinforces his political power and dynastic authority. His authority is given shape and form by the objects that vividly portray himself, his wealth, his learning, and his power to shape and control his own environment. The artist benefits from such an association by utilizing expensive materials and a competitive brief to produce innovative and multi-faceted art objects. Only now is it possible to look back at Federico's *studiolo*, admire its opulence and artistic skill, and reflect that ultimately, like the brilliantly inlaid décor, the claims of a provincial mercenary to dynastic power were a brilliant illusion.

Federico encouraged the artistic collaboration and international rivalry that became a feature of the art of the period. A Dalmatian (Luciano Laurana) designed the palace, a Venetian (Ambrogio Barocci) created the sculptures, a Florentine (Botticelli) designed the intarsia decoration for the *studiolo*, Piero della Francesca from Borgo and Justus from Ghent provided the paintings, and the Low Countries provided tapestries. Inspiration from the east is captured in Federico's attempt to emulate Mehmed the Conqueror's Topkapi Saray, his expensive Ottoman carpets, and Justus of Ghent's remarkably oriental paintings of Plato, Ptolemy, and Aristotle.

The material, political, and artistic exchanges that took place between east and west were crucial in shaping the art and architecture of the Renaissance. The art objects that resulted from these transactions were creations forged in the Renaissance bazaar of material exchanges, political alliances, and artistic collaborations that fulfilled a variety of religious, social, and political functions. Since the 19th century exchange and collaboration have been denigrated in favour of the celebration of the autonomous artistic genius, reluctant to sully his hands with such activities. To fully evaluate the artistic achievements of the Renaissance, it is necessary to acknowledge that the art that emerged from it was deeply imbued with the worlds of trade and politics, both of the east and of the west.

5. BRAVE NEW WORLDS

Putting Europe on the map

In 1482 a printing press in the German town of Ulm published a new edition of Ptolemy's *Geography*. Its world map (Fig. 25) captured what the world looked like to Europe's 15th-century ruling elite, from Henry VII in London to Mehmed the Conqueror in Constantinople. Ptolemy had written his *Geography* in Alexandria in the 2nd century AD. Arabic scholars had preserved and revised the text prior to its translation into Latin by the end of the 14th century. Medieval Christian geography had been limited to schematic maps, known as *mappae mundi*, which were religious

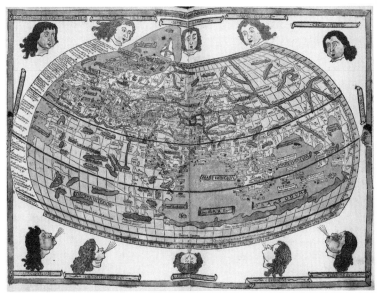

25.
Ptolemy's world map from one of the many new printed editions of his classical text *Geography*. This version was printed in Ulm in 1482.

symbols of the Christian understanding of creation. They placed Jerusalem at their centre, with little or no attempt to understand or represent the wider world. Ptolemy's *Geography* transformed 15th-century perceptions of the shape and size of the earth. His text listed and described over 8,000 places, as well as explaining how to draw regional and world maps. It undermined the medieval Christian belief in sacred, religious space. The grid of latitude and longitude that Ptolemy threw across the known world was secular and geometrical. This was the template used by the 15th- and 16th-century voyages of trade and discovery, which began to shape today's modern image of the globe, and which form the basis of this chapter.

For a 21st-century viewer, Ptolemy's world map still seems very unfamiliar. But for a late 15th-century ruler or merchant, the Ulm version of Ptolemy's map looked like a reasonably accurate representation of the world of the time. 'Europa' and the Mediterranean, 'Affrica' and 'Asia' are all quite recognizable. The centre of this world map lies to the east of mainland Europe, in Constantinople, Alexandria, and Baghdad. What seems erroneous to us today is the omission of the Americas, Australasia, the Pacific, the bulk of the Atlantic Ocean, and the southern tip of Africa (without which the Indian Ocean is represented as a giant lake). Ptolemy's world centred on the eastern Mediterranean and central Asia. These were the regions that represented the predominant geographical reality of educated people from the 2nd century AD right down to the close of the 15th century.

The *Geography* was an elite text, owned by princes, clerics, scholars, and merchants eager to display their own awareness of geography and travel through possession of expensive manuscript copies of Ptolemy. However, working maps from as early as the 14th century also reveal the mixed cultural traditions that constituted early Renaissance geography and travel. The anonymous Maghreb chart (Fig. 26), dated around 1330, is a practical example of the so-called 'portolan' charts used by merchants and navigators to move across the Mediterranean. The 'rhumb' lines that criss-cross the map are designed to aid compass bearings, allowing navigators to sail reasonably accurate courses. Produced in North Africa, it demonstrates the circulation of geographical knowledge, navigation skills, and trade between Christian and Muslim communities. Of its 202 place names, 48 are of Arabic origin, the rest Catalan, Hispanic, or Italian. Based on the expertise of Arab, Jewish, and Christian navigators and scholars, it was practical charts such as these that enabled the first tentative seaborne voyages beyond the bounds of Europe.

Rounding the Cape

In 1415 the Portuguese captured the Muslim city of Ceuta at the northern tip of Morocco. The victory gave Portugal a springboard for expansion down the West African coast. Previously marginalized at the westernmost point of Europe, 15th-century Portugal was a relatively poor, overwhelmingly agrarian country. Taking advantage of its geographical location facing out into the Atlantic, the Portuguese crown sought to break directly into the trans-Saharan trade routes, circumventing the need to pay crippling tariffs that burdened overland and seaborne trade routes via North Africa back into southern Europe. As the Portuguese crown claimed Madeira (1420), the Canary Islands (1434), the Azores (1439), and the Cape Verde Islands (1460s), the trade in

26.
This anonymous
sea chart, or
'portolan', is
known as the
'Maghreb chart'
and was drawn in
North Africa
around 1330. It
reveals how shared
knowledge and
resources
underpinned
Mediterranean
navigation.

basic materials like timber, sugar, fish, and wheat became more important than the glamorous search for gold. This led to a pragmatic redefinition of the aims of seaborne discovery and settlement on the part of the Portuguese crown.

Once they had settled the Azores, the Portuguese began sailing south into uncharted waters, or what was labelled on Ptolemy's map 'Terra Incognita'. Having reached the limit of Mediterranean traditions of navigation and map-making, the Portuguese employed the services of Jewish scholars to calculate the position of the sun, moon, and stars. Astrologer-geographers like Jafuda Cresques and Abraham Zacuto, both considered 'master astrologers, very knowledgeable of the routes according to the stars and the North Pole' developed solar tables, star charts, astrolabes, quadrants, and cross staffs. These were all designed to allow Portuguese navigators to calculate their latitude while sailing out of sight of land. While such innovations were not always successful, they did stimulate further voyages and more accurate maps. These included the Venetian cartographer Grazioso Benincasa's portolan chart of 1467 (Fig. 27). It shows the extent of Portuguese discoveries up to the mid-1460s, including Madeira, the Canaries, the Azores, and the recently discovered Cape Verde Islands. It also records coastal places of contact and commercial exchange. Benincasa's chart captures the extent to which Italian, German, and even French capital was investing in Portugal's newfound markets. The Portuguese crown was prepared to grant trading privileges to anyone, regardless of nationality, as long as they paid a percentage of all profits to the king. By the 1480s this agreement had become so successful that the Portuguese had rounded Sierra Leone and established trading posts (or *feitoria*) at São Jorge da Mina on the Guinea coast.

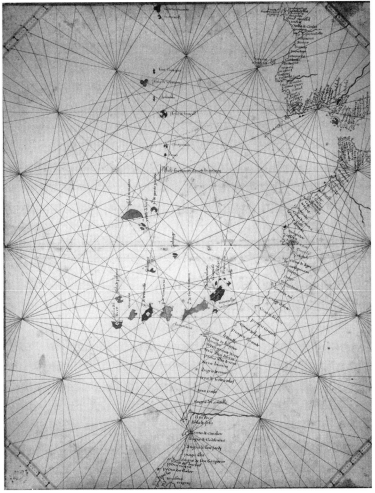

27. Grazioso Benincasa's portolan chart of West Africa (1467) is both a document of the most recent Portuguese discoveries and a new instrument of navigation and discovery in its own right.

Slowly but surely, such exchanges had a noticeable impact upon the culture and economy of communities in West Africa, Portugal, and the rest of mainland Europe. The mingling of people led to the creation of autonomous mixed-race communities in West Africa, referred to as *lançados*, who played

Portuguese off against Africans for their own commercial benefit. Copper, horses, and cloth were also traded for gold, malagueta pepper, carved ivory, and ebony. By the end of the 15th century approximately 30,000 ounces of gold were being shipped back to Lisbon, evading the overland routes back into Europe, and allowing Portugal to issue its first national gold coin, the *crusado*, as a symbol of its new-found wealth. Castile was also beginning to take notice of Portugal's profitable discoveries, and in 1475 unsuccessfully attempted to capture Portugal's Atlantic islands. The Treaty of Alcaçovas (1479) confirmed Portugal's territorial and commercial rights throughout the Atlantic Islands and West Africa, but this was just the first of many treaties signed between the two crowns as subsequent voyages opened up new territories and markets to the east and the west.

The 1480s saw increased enthusiasm for Portuguese seaborne exploration. Castile had been defeated, gold and exotic goods were flowing back into Lisbon, and the rest of Europe was looking at Portugal with increasing respect. In 1485 the Portuguese King John II wrote to Pope Innocent VIII boasting of 'the by no means uncertain hope of exploring the Barbarian Gulf', populated by 'kingdoms and nations of Asiatics, barely known among us'. John was referring to the Indian Ocean, claiming that the 'farthest limit of Lusitanian maritime exploration is at present only a few days distant from them, if the most competent geographers are but telling the truth'. This was a clever move by the king, ostensibly writing to the pope to express the hope that his navigators might find Indian communities in the east who 'practice very devoutly the most holy faith of the Saviour'. This religious motivation was subservient to the commercial benefits Portugal reaped from its African trade for decades, but it was helpful in obtaining papal support. The letter also announced the cultural and geographical achievements of Portugal's imminent discovery of a sea route into the Indian Ocean. Portuguese navigators were about to shatter Ptolemy's world picture, with its portrayal of a landlocked Indian Ocean, and their king wanted the world to know.

In December 1488 Bartolomeu Diaz returned to Lisbon to announce that he had sailed around the southernmost tip of Africa. A contemporary Portuguese geographer recorded that Diaz realized 'that the coast here turned northwards and northeastwards towards Ethiopia under Egypt and on to the Gulf of Arabia, giving great hope of the discovery of India'. As a result Diaz 'called it the "Cape of Good Hope"'. The news rendered printed maps still reproducing Ptolemy's view of the world increasingly obsolete. Henricus Martellus' world map of 1489 (Fig. 28) closely follows Ptolemy, up to its representation of southern Africa. The border of the map was clearly designed to show an endless African coastline. However, news of Diaz's voyage required the hasty addition of the Cape of Good Hope, and the revelation of the possibility of sailing into the Indian Ocean. In Martellus' map, Diaz's discovery breaks the established frame of European geographical awareness. From now on, European voyagers really were sailing into 'terra incognita', a whole New World where they could no longer rely on the classical authority of Ptolemy.

East is east

One observer who was particularly impressed by the Portuguese discoveries was the Genoese navigator Christopher Columbus,

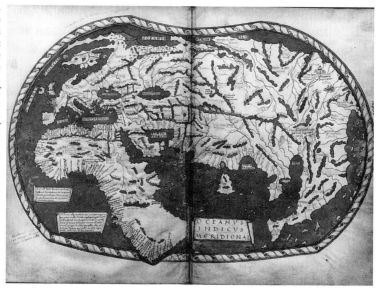

who was present at the Portuguese court when Diaz returned
with news of his circumnavigation of the Cape. It was Columbus'
observation of the practical achievements of the Portuguese navigators and his immersion in geographical writing from Ptolemy
to Marco Polo that led him to make a fateful decision. Columbus
uncritically accepted Ptolemy and Marco Polo's massive overestimation of the size of Asia. But he also realized that if
Ptolemy's estimate of the circumference of the world were cor-
rect, then a voyage to Asia that sailed westwards from Europe
would be much shorter than the south-eastern route followed by
the Portuguese. Columbus calculated that the westward distance
between Japan and the Azores was 3,000 miles. It was in fact
over 10,000 miles. Ptolemy's calculations on both the size of
Asia and the globe were wrong. If Columbus had known this, he
may never have embarked on his voyage in 1492.

It is easy to see the persuasiveness of Columbus' calculations by looking at Henricus Martellus' map and Martin Behaim's 1492 globe (Fig. 5). Both show a massively overextended Asian continent and potentially short voyage westwards from the Iberian Peninsula to Japan. Behaim's globe captures this possibility even more dramatically, and demonstrates how Columbus must have possessed a powerfully global picture of the shape and size of the world on the eve of his voyage. Columbus first proposed the idea to the Portuguese court in 1485, but his plan was turned down due to Lisbon's success in pursuing the sea route to the east via southern Africa. Instead Columbus took his proposal to the Castilian crown. In April 1492 they finally agreed to finance Columbus' voyage. Castile was in financial trouble after its disastrous campaign against the Portuguese and ongoing struggle against the Iberian Muslims. The possibility of cornering the market in spices and gold from the east was too good to miss. On 2 August 1492, Columbus finally departed on his first voyage from Palos in southern Spain, in command of 90 men in three ships, the *Niña*, the *Pinta*, and the *Santa Maria*.

After nearly two months sailing westwards across the Atlantic, on Thursday, 10 October, 'two hours after midnight land appeared'. Columbus had sighted the Bahamas, where he landed and encountered locals, who 'were all very well built, with very handsome bodies and very good faces', but were also ominously perceived to be 'good servants and of quick intelligence'. Columbus was impatient 'to leave for another very large island, which I believe must be Cipangu [Japan], according to the signs which these Indians whom I have with me make; they call it "Colba"'. Columbus was convinced that he was on the verge of reaching Japan. 'Colba' turned out to be Cuba. He skirted the coast of Cuba and Haiti, before wrecking his flagship and heading home with small traces of gold and several kidnapped 'Indians'.

Columbus' return to Europe caused a diplomatic storm. This was not because he had discovered a 'New World'—he still clung to the belief that he had reached the east by sailing west: Portugal objected that the Castilian-backed expedition broke the terms of the Treaty of Alcaçovas that guaranteed the Portuguese monopoly on all discoveries 'beyond Guinea'. But the ambiguity of this phrase, and the intercession of a sympathetic Spanish pope, granted the new discoveries to Castile under the terms of the Treaty of Tordesillas (1494). The treaty also stipulated that a map be drawn up with a line of partition defining the relative spheres of interest of the two crowns. The delegates agreed that 'a boundary or straight line be determined and drawn' running down the Atlantic, 'at a distance of three hundred and seventy leagues west of the Cape Verde Islands'. Everything to the west of this line belonged to Castile, everything to the east (and south) belonged to Portugal. Castile got what it believed was a new route to the east, while the Portuguese protected their African possessions and passage to the east via the Cape of Good Hope.

The jewel in the crown

The irony of Columbus' 'discovery' of America was that it was initially seen as a failure. Columbus appeared to have discovered a new territorial obstacle blocking the path to a shorter, commercially lucrative route to the east. The Portuguese, delayed in their attempt to capitalize on Diaz's discovery of the Cape by Columbus' voyage and the subsequent diplomatic dispute, despatched another expedition round the Cape with the explicit aim of reaching India. In July 1497 Vasco da Gama left Lisbon with 170 men in a fleet of four heavy ships, each carrying 20 guns and a variety of trade goods. Before rounding the Cape, da Gama's log records that the fleet spent an unprecedented 13 weeks out of sight of land. Da Gama now found himself in completely uncharted waters. Even worse, Portuguese navigational aids based on astronomical calculations were useless in the unfamiliar skies of the Indian Ocean.

Landing in Malindi, da Gama hired the services of an Arab navigator-astronomer, reputed to be one of the finest pilots of his time:

> Vasco da Gama, after he had a discussion with him, was greatly satisfied with his knowledge: principally, when he [the pilot] showed him a chart of the whole of the coast of India drawn, in the fashion of the Moors, that is with meridians and parallels . . . And when da Gama showed him a large astrolabe of wood which he had with him, and others of metal with which he measured the altitude of the sun, the pilot expressed no surprise, saying that some navigators of the Red Sea used brass instruments of triangular shape and quadrants with which they measured the altitude of the sun and principally of the Pole Star which they most commonly used in navigation.

These were techniques that were completely unknown to the European navigators. Jewish astronomical expertise had taken the Portuguese as far as the Cape. Now Islamic navigational skill would finally help them reach India.

Not only did the Arabic pilot provide da Gama with the navigational expertise required to sail across the Indian Ocean. He also unwittingly disclosed just how extensive the development of Arabic science and astronomy had become. Just as Ptolemy's classical texts on geography and astronomy had been transmitted from Alexandria to Constantinople, Italy, Germany, and Portugal, so they had also circulated eastwards via Damascus, Baghdad, Samarkand, and Hormuz. Mehmed the Conqueror's patronage of Ptolemy's *Geography* represented just one dimension of the vigorous tradition of Islamic astronomy and geography. In 1513 the Turkish naval commander known as Piri Reis issued a world map (Fig. 29) that its author claimed 'is based mainly on twenty charts and mappa mundi, one of which is drawn in the time of Alexander the Great, and is known as *dja'grafiye'*. This is clearly a reference to Ptolemy's *Geography*. Piri Reis goes on to explain his consultation of further practical charts. These included 'new maps of the Chinese and the Indian Seas', as well as 'one Arab map of India, four new Portuguese maps drawn according to the geometrical methods of India and China, and also the map of the western lands drawn by Columbus'. The Ottoman court in Istanbul was clearly keeping a close watch on developments in the western Atlantic.

Sadly, only the western portion of Piri Reis' map survives, but its detail suggests that the representation of the Indian Ocean would have been equally comprehensive in incorporating new Portuguese maps into the established astronomical and navigational expertise of Islamic, Hindu, and Chinese pilots and scholars. Piri Reis' comments also emphasize the extensive level of cultural exchange and circulation of knowledge that underpinned the Age of Discovery. Muslims, Hindus, and Christians were all trading information and ideas in an attempt to capture the political and commercial initiative. Such diffusion and exchange undoubtedly went back even further, as suggested by the survival of the so-called 'Kangnido' Korean world map (Fig. 30), made in 1402. This map clearly shows Chinese seaborne voyages to the Cape of Good Hope years before Diaz. It also

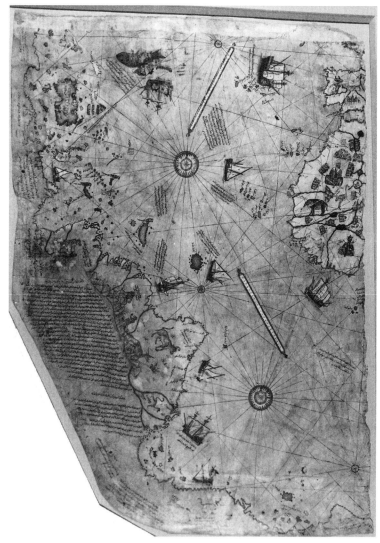

29.
Piri Reis' extremely
accurate world
map (1513) shows
the extent to which
geographical
information
circulated between
east and west. Its
missing eastern
portion was
presumably even
more detailed.

contains strong geographical affinities with Arabic and Ottoman
maps and charts, including the transcription of places names in
Africa and Europe taken from Arabic-Persian originals.

30.
The anonymous
'Kangnido' Korean
world map (1402)
shows a
circumnavigable
southern Africa,
suggesting that the
Portuguese were
not the first
seafaring nation to
'discover' the Cape
of Good Hope.

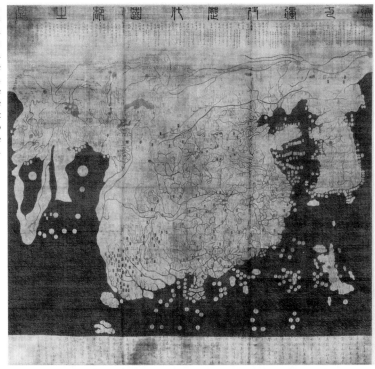

Navigationally speaking, da Gama and his expedition believed that they were sailing into a new world. They soon discovered that culturally they were entering a surprisingly familiar world in which they appeared to be alien, dirty, violent, poor, and technologically limited. Da Gama reached Calicut on the southern coast of India on 20 May 1498. The first person the expedition met was a Tunisian merchant, who greeted them with the exclamation in Spanish, 'May the Devil take you! What brought you here?' After travelling thousands of miles for nearly a year in an attempt to break the Islamic hold on the eastern trade in spices, this must have been a devastating encounter. Even worse, the gifts that da Gama had brought were more appropriate for trade in Guinea than ceremonial presentation to the elegant court of the Samorin of Calicut. When the local merchants saw da Gama's motley presentation of cloth, coral, sugar, oil, and honey, 'they laughed at it, saying it was not a thing to offer to a king, that the poorest merchant from Mecca, or from any other part of India gave more'. This inability to present suitable gifts produced political tensions and restricted the Portuguese to limited bartering. Nevertheless, the small but precious cargo of cinnamon, cloves, ginger, nutmeg, pepper, drugs, precious stones and woods that da Gama presented upon his return to Lisbon in September 1499 convinced the Portuguese court that they had finally broken into the spice trade.

Portugal's entry into the vast trading emporium of the Indian Ocean was no more than a drop in the ocean. The region's ritualized patterns of trade and exchange and the sheer magnitude and diversity of its commodities dwarfed the supply and demand of the early Portuguese fleets. The Portuguese responded with a pragmatic accommodation and acceptance of different methods of exchange, cynical exploitation of political differences between Hindu and Muslim communities, and the aggressive use of gunpowder to establish limited commercial footholds throughout the region. However, back in Europe maps, books, and diplomatic exchanges reported da Gama's voyage as the establishment of Portugal's monopolization of the Asian spice trade. King Manuel crisply informed his Castilian neighbour that 'the great trade which now enriches the Moors . . . shall, in consequence of our regulations be diverted to the nations and ships of our own kingdom'.

The Venetians were not so impressed at reports of da Gama's voyage. The merchant Girolamo Priuli vividly captured the commercial mood in Venice at the news: 'all the people from across the mountains who once came to Venice to buy spices with their money will now turn to Lisbon . . . because they will be able to buy at a cheaper price'. High prices in Venice were 'because the spices that come to Venice pass through all of Syria, and through the entire country of the Sultan and everywhere they pay the most burdensome duties . . . that a thing that cost one ducat multiplies to sixty and perhaps a hundred'. Priuli gloomily concluded, 'I clearly see the ruin of the city of Venice'.

The effect of the Portuguese commander's voyage was to transform the political map of the Renaissance world. Venice immediately attempted to sabotage discussions with Indian spice merchants who had arrived in Lisbon to discuss Portugal's role in the trade, and opened talks with both the Ottomans and the Egyptian Mamluks with the intention of using both diplomatic and even military force to defend their commercial interests. In 1511 Portugal responded by negotiating with the Persian ruler Shah Ismail for a joint military attack on Egypt, that would strangle Venice's spice supply and help Ismail in his war with the Ottomans. As is so often the case in the Renaissance, when trade and wealth were at stake, religious and ideological oppositions melted away.

As navigational information became a diplomatic and commercial bargaining counter, maps themselves became prized objects. They disclosed distant places and new commercial opportunities, and intimated that their owner understood the mysteries of long-distance travel and the acquisition of fabulous wealth. Maps were treated like the precious commodities to which they seemed to promise access. They were passports to wealth and power, all of which could be revealed to you in the safety of your study, without your ever needing to experience the danger and tedium of seaborne travel. By 1501 Venetian diplomats in Portugal were writing home promising to send 'maps both as far as Calicut and beyond'. Lisbon-based publishers surreptitiously sold commercially sensitive maps of the Portuguese routes to the east. One enterprising printer offered a map of 'the coast from India to Malacca and the map with the islands, because so far all the pilots are still busy in the king's house; but afterwards they are also at my disposition'. In 1502 Ercole d'Este's agent Albert Cantino paid a Portuguese geographer 12 gold ducats for the map known as the Cantino Planisphere (Fig. 31), which had to be smuggled out of Lisbon. The map traces da Gama's route to India and Pedro Cabral's discovery of Brazil in 1500, and also reproduces the line of demarcation agreed between Portugal and Castile under the terms of the Treaty of Tordesillas. It is also covered in detailed commercial information, from the description of the 'slaves and pepper and other things of much profit' in Guinea, to the 'spices and silks and brocades' to

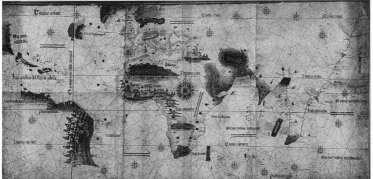

31.
The Cantino Planisphere was stolen from Lisbon in 1502 for its precious commercial information on the Portuguese sea route to the east. The line of demarcation agreed by the Treaty of Tordesillas runs through the Atlantic.

be found in Sumatra. The sketchy representation of the Americas reconfirms the enduring fascination with the impact of da Gama's expedition to the east, rather than Columbus' voyage to the west.

Global ventures

By 1502, the first major phase of seaborne travel had reached its climax. Ptolemy's world picture had been shattered and a recognizably modern image of the world had started to emerge. The Portuguese had rounded Africa, reached India, accidentally discovered Brazil *en route* to the east (1500), and were pushing on to Malacca (1511), Hormuz (1513), China (1514), and Japan (1543). To the west Columbus' three voyages to the Americas had established a thriving trade in gold, silver, and slaves. In four voyages undertaken between 1497 and 1502 Amerigo Vespucci conclusively proved that Columbus had discovered a new continent. Cleverly disseminating his discoveries via the printing press, Vespucci ensured that it would be him and not Columbus who became synonymous in the European imagination with this new continent, America. Castile now had a separate continent to claim as its own, and an empire to build that could rival its Iberian neighbour's.

With the revision of the European geographical imagination came a transformation in the texture of everyday life. The spices that flowed back into Europe affected what and how people ate, as did the influx of coconuts, oranges, yams, and bananas (from the east) and pineapples, groundnuts, papayas, and potatoes (from the Americas). The term 'spices' could also refer to a dizzying array of drugs (including opium, camphor, and cannabis), cosmetics, sugar, waxes, and cosmetics. Silk, cotton, and velvet changed what people wore, and musk and civet altered the way that they smelt. Dyes like indigo, vermilion, lac, saffron, and alum made Europe a brighter place, while porcelain, amber, ebony, sandalwood, ivory, bamboo, and lacquered wood all transformed the public and private domestic interiors of wealthy individuals. Tulips, parrots, rhinoceroses, chess sets, sexual appliances, and tobacco were just some of the more esoteric but significant goods that reached Europe from east and west. Lisbon itself was transformed into one of Europe's wealthiest cities: here it was possible to buy virtually anything and marvel at the monuments to the discoveries that drew on African and Indian motifs to create a beautiful hybrid architectural style. Princes displayed jewels, armour, statues, paintings, bezoar stones, and even parrots, monkeys, and horses in cabinets of curiosity, and Albrecht Dürer enthusiastically listed his acquisition of African salt cellars, Chinese porcelain, sandalwood, parrots, and Indian coconuts and feathers. If anything characterizes the nature of the European Renaissance, it is this complete transformation of all aspects of life to such an extent that is almost impossible to appreciate today.

By the first years of the 16th century, this transformation in taste had created an extremely lucrative market. Bigger ships known as carracks, mixing square and lateen (or triangular) sails and weighing up to 1000 tons, could sail further and carry more merchandise than ever before. Increasingly detailed maps and elaborate navigational instruments allowed merchants and rulers to finance evermore precise and ambitious commercial voyages. Politically the stakes were also getting higher as the Portuguese, Castilian, and French empires all vied for supremacy.

In 1513 the Portuguese finally reached the Moluccas, a small collection of islands in the Indonesian archipelago that provided the sole supply of cloves. This discovery provoked a serious political crisis. Since the Treaty of Tordesillas Portugal had pursued its commercial interests to the east, while Castile had concentrated on expansion to the west. This was fine when plotted on a flat map of the type obviously used under the terms of Tordesillas. But the discovery of the Moluccas posed the question of where such a line would fall in the eastern hemisphere if it were drawn all the way round the world on a globe.

Enter one particularly ambitious and far-sighted Portuguese pilot, Fernão de Magalhães, better known today as Ferdinand Magellan. He had sailed with the Portuguese fleet to Malacca in 1511, and suspected that a western passage to the Moluccas via the southern tip of South America would be shorter and quicker than the Portuguese route via the Cape of Good Hope. However, in reviving Columbus' original idea of reaching the east by sailing west, Magellan faced the perennial problem of Portuguese opposition to such a plan. He decided to offer the scheme to the Castilian king and future Hapsburg Emperor Charles V, putting forward a proposal that pointed out:

> It was not yet clearly ascertained whether Malacca was within the boundaries of the Portuguese or the Castilians, because hitherto its longitude had not been definitely known ... [but] it was absolutely certain that the islands called the Moluccas, in which all sorts of spices grow, and from which they were brought to Malacca, were contained in the western, Castilian division, and that it would be possible to sail to them and to bring the spices at less trouble and expense from their native soil to Castile.

Here was an ambitious commercial proposition that

required investment in a complex long-distance voyage, a typical example of the motivation for so many Renaissance voyages of 'discovery'. Nowhere in the primary material on Magellan is the circumnavigation of the globe ever discussed. Magellan's proposal was for a voyage that sailed westwards to the Moluccas, then came straight back via South America, avoiding the *Carreira da India*, the established Portuguese trade route to the east via the Cape of Good Hope. This was an operation that would claim the Moluccas for Castile on the basis of diplomatic and geographical precedent, cutting off Portugal's supply of top-quality spices and diverting Lisbon's wealth to Castile. Magellan's successful pitch for financial support was based on progressive global thinking. He arrived in Seville in 1519 with 'a well-painted globe showing the entire world, and thereon traced the course he proposed to take'. Globes, not maps, were now the objects that most accurately captured the political and commercial geography of the 16th-century world.

Magellan quickly convinced Castile. In September 1519 he set sail with five ships and 240 men. The voyage was unimaginably gruelling. Sailing down the coast of South America, Magellan had to suppress mutiny, and lost two ships searching for a way through the strait at the tip of South America that now bears his name. He then spent weeks sailing across a Pacific Ocean that was larger than his maps and globes had ever suggested. The exhausted fleet finally reached Samar in the Philippines in April 1521. Magellan embroiled himself in a petty local conflict, and on 27 April he was killed alongside forty of his men. The remnants of the dispirited fleet set sail again and finally reached the Moluccas where they loaded a substantial cargo of cloves, pepper, ginger, nutmeg, and sandalwood. Unable to face the planned return journey through Magellan's Strait, the crew agreed to return via the Cape of Good Hope, running the risk of capture by patrolling Portuguese ships. Their decision made global history. On 8 September 1522 just 18 of the original crew of 240 arrived back in Seville, having completed the first recorded circumnavigation of the globe.

The news of Magellan's voyage caused diplomatic uproar. Charles V immediately interpreted the voyage as a justification for claiming that the Moluccas lay within his half of the globe. His advisers began to build a diplomatic and geographical case for possession and 'urged that by mathematical demonstration and the judgement of men learned in that faculty it appeared that the Moluccas were within the limits of Castile'.

Both sides demanded diplomatic arbitration, but the political, commercial, and geographical complexities involved in apportioning the two halves of the globe involved years of complex negotiation. The Castilian team cleverly used classical authority to support their claim. Ptolemy's overestimation of the size of Asia ironically played into the hands of the Castilian claim to the Moluccas. By repeating the inaccurate width of Asia in their maps, Castile pushed the Moluccas further east, and thus into their half of the globe. The Castilians submitted maps and globes where 'the description and figure of Ptolemy and the description and model found recently by those who came from the spice regions are alike ... therefore Sumatra, Malacca and the Moluccas fall within our demarcation'. This mixture of classical scholarship and modern navigation proved irresistible.

Portugal hit back with its own array of maps, charts, and globes. Watching from the sidelines, the English merchant

Robert Thorne wrote to Henry VIII in 1527 on the extraordinary
game of geographical manipulation that passed for diplomacy:

> For these coasts and situation of the islands the cosmographers and
> pilots of Portugal and Spain do set after their purpose. The Spaniards
> move towards the Orient, because they should appear to appertain to
> the Emperor [Charles V]; and the Portuguese move toward the
> Occident, for that they should fall within their jurisdiction.

Castile's trump card in this game of cartographic poker was
the mapmaker Diogo Ribeiro. Like Magellan, Ribeiro had offered
his services to the Castilian crown in support of the Moluccas
voyage. As the two crowns sat down for their final attempt to
resolve the dispute at Saragossa in 1529, Ribeiro and his team of
cartographers constructed a series of maps and globes that placed
the Moluccas within the Castilian half of the globe. This was the
moment at which the Renaissance world went global in a recognizably modern sense. The Treaty of Tordesillas had been carried
out on a flat map, but the consequences of Magellan's voyage
meant that terrestrial globes suddenly became far more
convincing representations of the shape and scope of the world.

While such globes did not survive, Ribeiro's magnificent
world map dated 1529 (Fig. 32) remains as a remarkable testi-
mony to the manipulation of geographical reality that characterized the dispute over the Moluccas. Ribeiro placed the Moluccas
172 and a half degrees west of the Tordesillas line—just seven
and a half degrees inside the Castilian sphere. The map gave
Charles V the negotiating power he needed. Under the terms of
the Treaty of Saragossa, signed on 23 April 1529, Charles claimed
the enormous sum of 350,000 ducats from Portugal as compen-
sation for surrendering what he alleged were compelling geographical arguments in favour of his claim to the islands. He had

32.
Diogo Ribeiro's
comprehensive
1529 Planisphere
controversially
manipulated
contemporary
geographical
knowledge to place
the spice-
producing
Moluccas Islands
within the
Hapsburg half of
the globe. Ribeiro
was richly
rewarded for his
labours.

in fact realized that short-term cash was preferable to a long-term commercial investment, and that the cost and logistics of establishing a western trade route to the Moluccas were formidable. Portugal bought the islands, Charles paid off his creditors, and Ribeiro established himself as Castile's most respected cartographer. He guessed that his geographical sleight of hand would never be discovered, because without an accurate method for calculating longitude, it would be impossible to ever fix the exact position of the Moluccas. He also contributed to the creation of the geographical perception of the two hemispheres. This was not based on any geographical reality, but on the commercial conflict between Portugal and Castile, which as one contemporary commentator remarked, was only resolved 'by dint of cunning and cosmography'.

New worlds, old stories

Charles V also had another reason for withdrawing from the dispute over the Moluccas. With Columbus' discovery of America, the gold and silver that had started to flow back into the coffers of Charles's Hapsburg Empire began to dwarf the revenue of the eastern spice trade. Portugal had established a string of hybrid trading posts throughout the east, which demanded pragmatic forms of trade and exchange that often revealed the limitations of European culture. Spain on the other hand used its military power to turn America into one large slave and mining colony.

Having established settlements on a number of the Caribbean islands, in particular Hispaniola and Cuba, the Spanish sought more lucrative financial rewards from the mainland. In 1521 Hernando Cortes reached Tenochtitlán (modern-day Mexico City), the capital of the Aztec empire; this he systematically destroyed, killing most of its inhabitants in the process, including its emperor, Montezuma. In 1533 the adventurer Francisco Pizarro led a handful of *conquistadores* and horses in the occupation of Cuzco (now in modern Peru), the capital of the Incan empire. The indigenous population had little commercial or military power to oppose the violent depredations of the Spaniards, who imposed a quasi-feudal arrangement upon conquered regions, known as *encomienda*. This involved the division of small local communities amongst Spanish overseers, who provided a brutally exploitative 'livelihood' (in effect exacting unpaid hard labour) and Christian education. Rather than moving forward as a result of discovery, the Spanish seemed to be moving backwards into the Middle Ages.

In their encounter with a New World, the early voyagers and *conquistadores* looked for models from the Old World to understand the cultures it confronted. In the case of Columbus and his successors, this involved comparing New World inhabitants with the Muslims who had been expelled from Spain, along with the Jewish population, just before Columbus set sail on his first voyage in 1492. This early example of 'ethnic cleansing' seems to have been carried over in the psychological baggage that subsequent Spanish adventurers took with them across the Atlantic. Cortes compared the dwellings and inhabitants of Tenochtitlán to 'those of Granada when that city was captured', and referred to the Aztec temples as 'mosques'. The *Requirimiento*, the speech read out by Spanish commanders when claiming control over territories and peoples in the New World, was based on the document used to demand the submission of Muslims during the Castilian *reconquista*. Spain exported its military aggression and religious intolerance of Islam to the New World, a process that only magnified misunderstanding and encouraged violence. Blinded by greed and terrified by the cultural difference they experienced, the Spanish systematically wiped out both the Incan and Aztec cultures, two of the most advanced civilizations that the pre-modern world had ever seen.

Conservative estimates calculate that of a world population of approximately 400 million in 1500, roughly 80 million inhabited the Americas. By 1550, the population of the Americas had been slashed to around ten million. At the start of the 16th century Mexico's population has been estimated at 25 million. In 1600, it had been reduced to one million. European diseases such as smallpox and measles wiped out most of the indigenous population, but warfare, slaughter, and terrible treatment also accounted for a huge number of fatalities. The romance of discovering piles of gold and silver had quickly turned into a dirty, murderous business of mining and enslavement.

The Spanish exploitation of the Americas had a direct impact on the economy of Europe. Initially, gold flowed back into Europe from Hispaniola and Central America. However, the conquests of Mexico and Peru soon tipped the balance in favour of silver mining. Between 1543 and 1548 silver deposits were found at Zacatecas and Guanajuato north of Mexico City; in 1543 the Spaniards discovered the infamous sugarloaf mountain of silver at Potosí in Bolivia. The decisive breakthrough came in 1555 with the discovery of the mercury amalgamation process, which allowed the creation of much purer silver through the smelting of silver ore with mercury. The result was a massive influx of silver into Europe. By the end of the 16th century over 270,000 kg of silver and approximately 2,000 kg of gold were reaching Europe every year, compounding the rise in inflation, and thereby contributing to what economic historians have called a 'price revolution', as wages and the cost of living soared, providing the framework for the long-term development of European capitalism.

This boom had a more sinister dimension. The American mines and estates required workers, and the decimation of the local population soon meant that the Spanish needed another source of labour. Their solution was slaves. In 1510 King Ferdinand of Castile authorized the export of 50 African slaves, 'the best and strongest available' to the mines of Hispaniola. Alonso Zuazo wrote from there to Charles V in 1518, concerned at the work rate of the Indians. He recommended the 'import of *negros*, ideal people for the work here, in contrast to the natives, who are so feeble that they are only suitable for light work'. Between 1529 and 1537 the Spanish crown issued 360 licences to carry slaves from Africa to the New World. Thus began one of the most ignominious features of the Renaissance, as African slaves, kidnapped or bought for 50 pesos each by Portuguese 'merchants' in West Africa, were crammed into boats and shipped to the New World. There they were sold for double their purchase price and set to work in mines and on estates. Between 1525 and 1550 approximately 40,000 slaves were shipped from Africa to the Americas, enriching European merchants and crowns: it should be remembered that the price of many of the great achievements of the period was misery, persecution, and death.

Not all Spaniards endorsed the horrific slaughter and oppression that took place in the Americas. The Franciscan Fray Motolinia believed that 'if anyone should ask what has been the cause of so many evils, I would answer: covetousness'. Bartolomé de Las Casas similarly argued, 'I do not say that they want to kill them [Indians] directly, from the hate they bear them; they kill them because they want to be rich and have much gold'. Philosophically, the discovery of a New World also transformed European understanding of its own cultural superiority. In 'On the Cannibals', published in his *Essays* of 1580, the humanist Michel de Montaigne claimed to have spoken at length with several Brazilian Indians. He concluded 'there is nothing savage or barbarous about those peoples, but that every man calls barbarous anything that he is not accustomed to'. Montaigne developed a highly sceptical and relativistic approach to perceptions of 'civilization' and 'barbarism', arguing that 'we can indeed call those folk barbarians by the rules of reason but not in comparison with ourselves, who surpass them in every kind of barbarism'.

The discovery of America had revolutionized Renaissance Europe's world picture. It had confounded deeply entrenched classical philosophical and religious beliefs that simply could not accommodate the existence of the culture, language, and belief systems of the indigenous inhabitants. It was partly responsible for defining Europe's shift from a medieval world to a more recognizably modern world. However, the discovery of America brought together a volatile fear of the new and the unknown, with a desire for unlimited wealth that ignored the incredible suffering and oppression inflicted upon indigenous people and slaves in the Americas. Its legacy can still be seen in the poverty and political instability of much of South America today, and the crippling inequalities of wealth and opportunity that characterize so much of the modern global economy.

In 1565 a Spanish galleon laden with cinnamon sailed from Manila to Mexico, finally linking up Spain's American colonies with the markets of south-east Asia. If there is one moment from which the emergence of the modern global economy can be dated, it is surely here. Europe's initial desire to reach the markets of the east had finally led to the creation of a global marketplace and a price revolution that would transform the continent forever. Sadly, in its quest for the wealth of the east, Europeans came to denigrate the communities that they encountered in Asia, Africa, and the Americas, and proceeded to impose a regime of colonial domination, which was to take centuries to build and which is only finally being dismantled today.

6. Experiments, dreams, and performances

> Come, Mephistopheles, let us dispute again,
> And reason of divine astrology.
> Speak, are there many spheres above the moon?
> Are all celestial bodies but one globe,
> As is the substance of this centric earth?

Faustus, in Christopher Marlowe, *Doctor Faustus, c.*1592

Christopher Marlowe's *Doctor Faustus* dramatizes the excitement and danger associated with the rise of science in the Renaissance. Faustus is a learned 'astrologer' who has reached the limits of the study of astronomy and anatomy. In seeking magical powers of life over death, Faustus sells his soul to the devil Mephistopheles. Given a chance to repent, he refuses. He is more interested in questioning Mephistopheles on the controversial topic of 'divine astrology'. Faustus is ultimately damned and falls to hell. But his preference for learning and contempt for religion caught the late Renaissance popular imagination. His fate encapsulates modern anxieties about the ethics of scientific experimentation. This ambivalence (we want to know, but can we know too much?) captures the mood of the transformations in popular and applied science that took place in the 15th and 16th centuries. The individual's relationship to his/her mind, body, and environment were all transformed as a result of renewed scientific collaboration in the pursuit of practical problem-solving, exchanges of ideas between cultures, and the impact of new technologies such as printing. This chapter explores this scientific transformation, and shows that changing perceptions of time, space, and the body were also rapidly incorporated into the philosophy and literature of the time.

From macrocosm to microcosm

Once Faustus has sold his soul, he asks Mephistopheles for a book 'where I might see all characters and planets of the heavens'. The most controversial book that Faustus could have consulted was *On the Revolutions of the Celestial Spheres* by the Polish canon and astronomer Nicolaus Copernicus (Fig. 33). First printed in Nuremberg in May 1543, Copernicus' revolutionary book overturned the medieval belief that the earth lay at the centre of the universe. Copernicus' vision of the heavens showed that the earth, along with all the other known planets, rotated around the sun. Copernicus subtly revised the work of classical Greek and Arabic astronomy scholars. He argued that 'they did not achieve their aim, which we hope to reach by accepting the fact that the earth moves'.

Copernicus' attempt to limit the revolutionary significance of his ideas by accommodating them within a classical scientific tradition failed. The Catholic Church was horrified and condemned the book. Luther also angrily denounced Copernicus, exclaiming, 'This fool wants to turn the entire art of astronomy upside down'. Copernicus' argument overturned the biblical belief that the earth—and humanity with it—was at the centre of the universe. This was a dangerous but liberating idea: the individual adrift in a meaningless universe, free from the divine order imposed by the church.

Within a month of the publication of Copernicus' treatise, another book was printed that would revolutionize another area

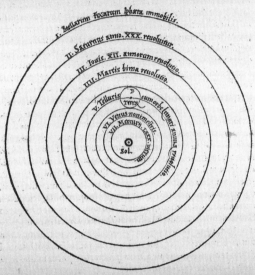

NICOLAI COPERNICI

net, in quo terram cum orbe lunari tanquam epicyclo contineri diximus. Quinto loco Venus nono mense reducitur. Sextum deniqʒ locum Mercurius tenet, octuaginta dierum spacio circū currens. In medio uero omnium residet Sol. Quis enim in hoc

I. Stellarum fixarum sphæra immobilis.
II. Saturnus anno. XXX. reuoluitur.
III. Iouis. XII. annorum reuolutio.
IIII. Martis bima reuolutio.
V. Telluris cum orbe lunari annua reuolutio.
VI. Venus nonimestris.
VII. Mercurii LXXX. dierum.
Sol.

pulcherimo templo lampadem hanc in alio uel meliori loco po neret, quàm unde totum simul possit illuminare? Siquidem non inepte quidam lucernam mundi, alij mentem, alij rectorem uo= cant. Trimegistus uisibilem Deum, Sophoclis Electra intuentē omnia. Ita profecto tanquam in solio regali Sol residens circum agentem gubernat Astrorum familiam. Tellus quoqʒ minime fraudatur lunari ministerio, sed ut Aristoteles de animalibus ait, maximā Luna cū terra cognationē habet. Concipit interea à Sole terra, & impregnatur annuo partu. Inuenimus igitur sub hac

of science: Andreas Vesalius' *On the Structure of the Human Body.* Published in Basle in June 1543, Vesalius' book marked the beginning of modern observational science and anatomy. Its dramatic title page (Fig. 34) depicts Vesalius conducting a graphic public anatomy lesson, held in a Palladian-style 'theatre', surrounded by students, citizens, and fellow physicians. Vesalius calmly returns our gaze as he peels back the female cadaver's abdomen. This gesture voyeuristically invites the reader to open the book and follow the anatomist as he reduces the human body to the skeleton that hovers above the dissected body. Vesalius revealed the mystery of the inner body as a complex map of flesh, blood, and bone, a potentially infinite source of study. His exploration of the secrets of the human body opened the way for the later 16th-century study of the ear, the female reproductive organs (including the partially understood discovery of the Fallopian tubes in 1561), the venous system, and, in 1628, William Harvey's theory of the circulation of the blood.

Like Copernicus, Vesalius' anatomical studies were based on methodical observation and analysis. For Copernicus, this meant gazing at the stars through scientific instruments of his own invention. For Vesalius it meant stealing the bodies of the condemned and the diseased, to which he confessed: 'I was not afraid to snatch in the middle of the night what I so longed for'. While Vesalius discovered the microscopic secrets of the human body, Copernicus explored the macrocosmic mysteries of the universe. The implications were profound. Copernicus ultimately transformed scientific apprehensions of time and space by undermining the notion of a divinely ordered world awaiting the final biblical Day of Judgement. Instead, the earth was envisaged as one planet amongst the vast, empty time and space of the universe. Vesalius envisaged the individual as an infinitely complex and intricate mechanism of blood, flesh, and bone that Shakespeare's Hamlet would later regard as a 'quintessence of

34.
The title page to
Andreas Vesalius'
*On the Structure of
the Human Body*
(1543), where the
drama of
anatomical
dissection is
carried out as if in a
theatre.

dust' and the philosopher René Descartes would call a 'moving machine'. Both formulations would be used to repeatedly undermine established religious conceptions of 'man'.

Alongside Copernicus and Vesalius came hundreds of publications that began to define the emerging disciplines of scientific enquiry: mathematics, physics, biology, the natural sciences, and geography. In mathematics, Luca Pacioli's *Everything about Arithmetic, Geometry and Proportion* (1494) was the first account of the practical application of arithmetic and geometry, one of 214 mathematical books published in Italy between 1472 and 1500. In 1545 the astrologer Geronimo Cardano published his *Great Art*, the first contemporary European book of algebra. In 1537 Niccolò Tartaglia issued his *New Science*, dealing with physics, followed by his study of arithmetic, *A General Treatise on Numbers and Measurement* (1556). In the natural sciences Leonhard Fuchs' botanical work *History of Plants* (1542) studied over 500 plants. Conrad Gesner's multi–volume *History of Animals* (1551–8) contained hundreds of illustrations that redefined zoology. In geography experiments in new ways of mapping the world culminated in Gerard Mercator's 1569 world map: his famous projection is still used today.

Scientific innovation was invariably tied to practical requirements, and nowhere more than in the field of warfare. Niccolò Tartaglia's early publications on mechanics, dynamics, and motion were in fact the first modern studies of ballistics. His *Various Queries and Inventions* (1546) was dedicated to the militarily ambitious Henry VIII, and deals with ballistics as well as the creation and use of artillery, gunpowder, and bombs. Tartaglia's work responded to and further developed new inventions in weaponry and warfare, from the innovation of using gunpowder as a propellant in the early 14th century, to the emergence of cavalry as a decisive factor in early 16th-century conflict. The impact of such military-scientific developments led to further advancements in the fields of anatomy and surgery. In 1545 Ambroise Paré, a great admirer of Vesalius, published his study of surgery based on his involvement in the Franco-Hapsburg wars of the 1540s. Paré disproved the popular belief that gunshot wounds were poisonous and rejected the use of dressing wounds in boiling oil, a practical innovation that subsequently earned him the epithet of the father of modern surgery.

Science in the marketplace

In mathematics theoretical developments were intimately related to changes in international trade, finance, and the arts. Luca Pacioli's book drew on Arabic treatises on arithmetic, geometry, and proportion to provide merchants with the first systematic account of double-entry bookkeeping. Jacopo de' Barbari's *Portrait of Fra Luca Pacioli with a Young Man* (1494) (Fig. 35) exemplifies how Pacioli straddled science, religion, art, and scholarship in popularizing his work. In Barbari's painting, Pacioli consults a printed edition of the Greek mathematician Euclid's *Elements*, which he illustrates by drawing an equilateral triangle inside a circle. This application of Euclidean geometry is represented by the dodecahedron that rests on a copy of Pacioli's *Summa*, and the remarkable semi-regular glass polyhedron suspended from above. Pacioli required the help of artists like Barbari and Leonardo to visualize his practical investigations into mathematics and geometry, while they learnt from Pacioli to use his theoretical grasp of proportion, perspective, and optics.

35.
With its precise use of geometrical symbols and objects, Jacopo de' Barbari's *Portrait of Fra Luca Pacioli* (1494) captures the creative alliance between art and science.

Geometry and mathematics provided new ways of understanding the increasingly elaborate and often invisible movement of commodities and paper money across the globe, but they also enabled new developments in ship design, surveying, and map-making, which anticipated ever more rapid commercial transactions of a speed and volume hitherto unimaginable. Regiomontanus' book *On Triangles* became crucial to 16th-century map-makers and navigators. Its sophisticated treatment of spherical trigonometry allowed cartographers to construct terrestrial globes and map projections that took into account the curvature of the earth's surface. The first printed edition of Regiomontanus' book was published in 1533 in Nuremberg, the home of the early terrestrial globe industry that emerged in the aftermath of the first circumnavigation of the globe in 1522.

Scientific innovation in mathematics, astronomy, and geometry enabled increasingly ambitious long-distance travel and commercial exchange both eastwards and westwards, which in itself created new opportunities as well as new problems. Encountering new people, plants, animals, and minerals throughout Africa, south-east Asia, and the Americas enlarged and redefined the domains of European physiology, botany, zoology, and mineralogy. These developments often had a more specifically commercial dimension. Agricola's *De re metallica*, first published in 1556, dealt with 'Digging of ore', 'Smelting', 'Separation of silver from gold, and of lead from gold and silver', and the 'Manufacture of salt, soda, alum, vitriol, sulphur, bitumen, and glass'. The combination of chemistry, mineralogy, and Agricola's observations and experiences of the mining communities of southern Germany revolutionized mining techniques, and played a crucial role in the massive increase in the production and export of New World silver in the latter half of the 16th century.

Merchants and financiers soon realized that investing in science could be a profitable business. In 1519 the German humanist Ulrich von Hutton wrote a treatise on guaiacum, a new wonder drug from the Americas that was believed to cure syphilis. Dedicating his book to the Archbishop of Mainz, Hutton wrote, 'I hope that Your Eminence has escaped the pox but should you catch it (Heaven forbid but you can never tell) I would be glad to treat and heal you'. It was believed (mistakenly) that syphilis originated in the New World and returned to Europe with Columbus in 1493, and that the geographical origin of the disease had to provide the cure. In 1530 the physician and poet Girolamo Fracastoro christened the disease in his classically inspired poem 'Syphilis', which extolled the curative powers of guaiacum. The German merchant house of Fugger, which held an import monopoly on the drug, began a campaign to endorse guaiacum, opening a chain of hospitals exclusively supplying the drug. As the price climbed and its uselessness became apparent, the Swiss physician and alchemist Paracelsus published a series of attacks on guaiacum, denouncing it as a commercial scam, and recommending the more painful use of mercury. The Fuggers responded by using their financial muscle to suppress Paracelsus' publications and ridicule his scientific credibility. The ethically dubious world of patent medicines was born.

The measure of time

The preceding examples reveal how scientific enquiry often responded to very specific social requirements. But the commissioning of new areas of scientific research could often have more far-reaching and occasionally unfortunate consequences for its patron. Copernicus' findings came out of his employment by the papacy to work on the reform of the so-called Julian calendar, which was first established by the Romans in 45BC. This calendar was based on an inaccurate measurement of the length of a year, which meant that over the centuries the dates on the calendar fell out of step with the autumn and spring equinoxes. This was particularly alarming for the church, which required consistency in the dates of its religious rites and festivals, especially Easter. Calendar reform had been discussed for centuries, but at the Fifth Lateran Council (1512–17) Copernicus was asked to propose revisions on the basis of his astronomical observations. Rather than redefining the church's temporal power, he inadvertently ended up undermining it by his conclusion that the earth moved round the sun. The calendar was finally reformed under Pope Gregory XIII in 1582, when Catholic Europe went to sleep on the night of 4 October and woke up the next morning on 15 October. Not surprisingly Protestant Europe refused to accept the Catholic calendar until 1700.

By the mid-16th century the measurement of time had become a complex public issue as it organized everyday life, and its accuracy and standardization became increasingly important. Water clocks had already been used in China and Islam for centuries, and weight-driven mechanical clocks began to appear in Europe in the late 13th century. By the beginning of the 15th century German inventors strove for greater accuracy and standardization of time with their spring-driven clocks. Town clocks and elaborate personal watches began to create a heightened awareness of the mechanised, secular passage of time. The Christian perception of time was based on prefiguration: all of life was just counting down to the Day of Judgement. Secular clock time created a new rhythm of circular, repetitious time, controlled by man-made mechanisms rather than God. Petrarch told Emperor Charles IV that time 'is so precious, nay so estimable a possession, that it is the one thing that the learned agree can justify avarice'. Time, like money, became quantifiable. Day-to-day urban life increasingly required clock time as a basic principle of social organization.

Science from the east

Renaissance science also received added impetus from the increased transmission of knowledge between east and west. From the late 14th century, classical Greek scientific texts started to reach Europe from the Byzantine Empire. Many of these texts had survived in Arabic, Persian, and Hebrew translations which had been subject to vigorous revision in centres of learning such as Toledo in Spain and the Academy of Science established in Baghdad in the 9th century by its caliph, al-Ma'mūn. Islamic centres of learning were crucial in driving forward scientific advances based on both Greek learning and Arabic innovations particularly in the fields of medicine and astronomy. As early as the 1140s Hugo of Santalla, a Latin translator of Arabic texts wrote, 'it befits us to imitate the Arabs especially, for they are as it were our teachers and the pioneers'.

Arabic studies of medicine directly affected the dissemination of knowledge in the west. The 10th-century Arabic scholar Avicenna (Ibn-Sīnā) studied the Greek medical treatises of Galen and Aristotle in composing his encyclopaedic book the *Canon of Medicine*, where he defined medicine as 'the science by which we learn the various states of the human body, when in health and when not in health, whereby health is conserved and whereby it is restored after being lost'. The *Canon* was one of 80 Arabic texts translated into Latin in Toledo in the 12th century by Gerard of Cremona. Gerard's translation generated over 30 editions of the *Canon* printed in Italy between 1500 and 1550, as Avicenna's book became a set medical text in universities throughout Europe. In 1527 the Venetian physician Andrea Alpago published a new edition of the *Canon* based on his experience as physician to the Venetian consulate in Damascus. Alpago also studied the writings of the Syrian physician Ibn al-Nafis (1213–88), whose research on the pulmonary movement of the blood influenced 16th-century European investigation of circulation. Vesalius condemned academic physicians who spent their time 'unworthily decrying Avicenna and the rest of the Arabic writers'. He was so convinced of the importance of Arabic medicine that he began to learn the language himself, and wrote commentaries praising the therapeutics and materia medica of al-Rāzī ('Rhazes'). In 1531 Otto Brunfels, the so-called 'father of botany', edited a printed edition of the 9th-century materia medica of Ibn Sarābiyūn (Serapion the younger), which had a decisive influence on his own understanding of botany.

In astronomy and geography Arabic influence was even more pronounced. Arabic scholars were particularly instrumental in translating the crucial works of the Greek cosmographer Ptolemy. His *Almagest* and *Geography* were translated from Greek into Arabic, criticized, and then revised in Toledo, Baghdad, and Samarkand. In 1175 Gerard of Cremona translated the *Almagest* from Arabic into Latin, and the *Geography* was translated from Greek into Latin at the beginning of the 15th century. After the fall of Constantinople in 1453, the Ottoman Sultan Mehmed the Conqueror proved to be an enthusiastic patron of Ptolemy. In his chronicle *The History of Mehmed the Conqueror* (1467) the Greek scholar Kritovoulos of Imbros recounted one particular instance of Mehmed's cosmopolitan, polyglot patronage of cartography:

> His Highness the Sultan used to read philosophical works translated into the Arabic from Persian and Greek, and discuss the subjects which they treated with the scholars of his court. Having read the

works of the renowned geographer Ptolemy and perused the diagrams which explained these studies scientifically, the Sultan found
these maps to be in disarray and difficult to construct. Therefore he
charged the philosopher [Georgius] Amirutzes with the task of drawing a new clearer and more comprehensible map. Amirutzes
accepted with pleasure, and worked with meticulous care. After
spending the summer months in study and research, he arranged the
sections in scientific order . . . having completed his studies he presented the Sultan and those engaged in scholarship and science with
a work of great benefit. Amirutzes wrote the names of the regions and
cities in the Arabic script.

Amirutzes' map (Fig. 36) is an amalgamation of Ptolemy's
calculations with more up-to-date Arabic, Greek, and Latin geographical information. With south oriented at its top, scales of
latitude, and a complex conical projection, this was a cutting-edge
world map. Mehmed's enthusiastic patronage made Istanbul a

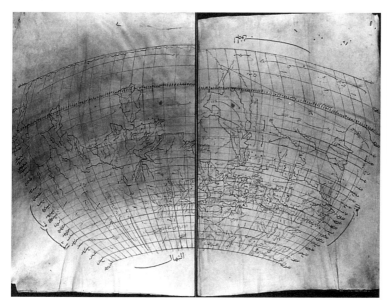

36.
Mehmed the
Conqueror
commissioned
Georgius
Amirutzes'
beautiful
Ptolemaic map
c.1465. It shows
how the study of
Ptolemy developed
in the east as well
as in the west.

centre of Ptolemy studies that involved exchanges between east and west, as has already been seen in the careers of George of Trebizond and Francesco Berlinghieri.

Scientific transactions between east and west also contributed to Copernicus' account of the heliocentric nature of the solar system. One of the most important centres of Arabic astronomy and mathematics was established at the Maragha observatory in Persia in the mid-13th century. Its leading figure was Nasir ad-Din aṭ-Ṭūsī (1201–74) whose *Memoir on Astronomy* (*Tadhkira fī'ilm al'haya*) modified Ptolemy's contradictory work on the motion of the spheres. Tusi's most important revision of Ptolemy led to the creation of the 'Tusi couple' (Fig. 37). This theorem states that linear motion can be derived from uniform circular motion, which Tusi demonstrated using one sphere rolling inside another of twice the radius. Historians of astronomy have

37.
Nasir ad-Dîn aṭ-Ṭūsī's illustration of his theorem the 'Tusi couple' from his mid-13th-century *Memoir on Astronomy*. The theorem decisively influenced Copernicus' development of his heliocentric vision of the solar system.

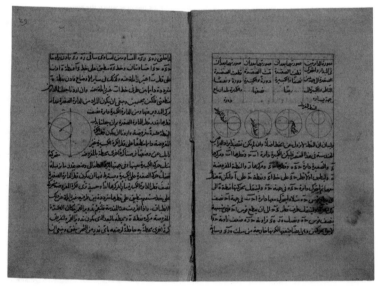

now realized that Copernicus reproduced the Tusi couple in his *Revolutions*, and that the theorem was crucial in defining his heliocentric vision of the solar system. Nobody looked for Arabic influence upon Copernicus and his European contemporaries, because the assumption was that there was nothing to find. It is unclear how Copernicus learnt of at-Tūsi's work, but this example of the direct influence of Arabic science upon European astronomy suggests that even more discoveries await scholars prepared to investigate the vigorous but now neglected exchange of ideas that took place between east and west.

Science goes to press

One of the reasons that information on many of these exchanges has been lost is that European science embraced the advent of the printing press, whereas, primarily for religious reasons, Islam was reluctant to adopt the new invention. In Europe, print did not simply provide a convenient outlet for new scientific ideas: it drove science forward by supplying features that manuscripts could not provide. Modern scientific analysis is based on the principles of observation, experimentation, comparison, standardization, and dissemination. These principles were impossible within a manuscript culture. Scientists could not compare and contrast notes on standard scientific works as no two manuscripts were ever the same.

Print changed all this. It made possible the standardization of texts as well as symbols, numbers, and figures. It created scientific communities by bringing together university teachers, printers, artists, translators, and freelance scholars in the printing of textbooks, as well as cutting-edge monographs on the new science. Printing also allowed scholars to systematically analyse the classical scientific texts of Ptolemy, Aristotle, Averroës, and Avicenna. It facilitated the collation and comparison of different manuscripts of a particular scientific text, which led to the correction of mistakes and the pooling of new ideas. Copernicus and Vesalius both began their scientific careers by translating and editing classical scientific texts before publishing their own new studies. They saw no inconsistency in editing Ptolemy and Galen and then printing treatises that appeared to contradict their classical predecessors. This was a strategic way of legitimizing their own ideas, but it also reflected a genuine respect for many of the insights of the classics.

Vesalius captured the importance of print in shaping science in a letter to the printer of his *Fabrica*, Johannes Oporinus. 'Special care should be employed', Vesalius specifies, 'on the impression of the plates which are not to be printed like ordinary textbooks with simple line engravings': light, shade, and artistry must be employed to maximize the relationship between word and image. Vesalius underlined his point by recounting the success of one of his earlier publications, which a colleague admired because he was 'able to observe the construction of man better from my plates than from the dissection of the human fabric'. The printed word had taken on greater authority and clarity than the body itself.

The art of science

The printing press brought together art and science as never before, and one of the individuals that capitalized on this situation was Albrecht Dürer. He quickly mastered the new technique of copperplate engraving, and in 1506 he travelled to Italy 'to learn the secrets of the art of perspective'. He had become convinced that what he regarded as 'the new art must be based upon science—in particular, upon mathematics, as the most exact, logical, and graphically constructive of the sciences'. In 1525 he published a treatise on geometry and perspective entitled *A Course in the Art of Measurement with Compass and Ruler*, which he hoped would 'benefit not only the painters but also goldsmiths, sculptors, stonemasons, carpenters and all those who have to rely on measurement'.

Dürer's book carefully explained the application of the new science of perspective and optics. It also contained illustrations of 'drawing machines' that could be used to impose the grid of perspective upon the subject. One of the most infamous of these illustrations shows the draughtsman using a sight to locate his subject on a piece of paper (Fig. 38). The grid-like structure of the artist's plate corresponds to the glass panel that separates draughtsman from model. The draughtsman simply copies every point on the glass onto the corresponding grid reference on his plate. The subject is a reclining naked woman, at the mercy of the voyeuristic, controlling gaze of the artist. Dürer's illustration

38.
Science or voyeurism? Dürer's draughtsman gazing at a naked woman through a 'drawing machine', from his *Course in the Art of Measurement*, printed in 1525.

shares many similarities with the female cadaver whose womb is ripped open for the edification of a roomful of men in Vesalius' *Fabrica*. For both Dürer and Vesalius, women have no part to play in this artistic and scientific revolution, other than as objects for dissection or mute, sexually available models.

An early influence on Dürer's career was the figure who has come to personify the relations between art and science in the Renaissance: Leonardo da Vinci. Luca Pacioli claimed that Leonardo was the 'most worthy of painters, perspectivists, architects and musicians, one endowed with every perfection', who utilized his immersion in science to market his skills as a sculptor, surveyor, military engineer, and anatomical draughtsman. Leonardo's ability to combine artistic skills with practical scientific ability made his services highly prized by several powerful patrons.

In 1482 Duke Ludovico Sforza of Milan employed Leonardo as a military engineer on the basis of a curriculum vitae that emphasized his practical (and destructive) abilities:

> I have plans for very light, strong and easily portable bridges . . . I have methods for destroying every fortress . . . I will make canon, mortar and light ordnance . . . I will assemble catapults, mangonels, trebuckets and other instruments . . . I believe I can give complete satisfaction in the field of architecture, and the construction of both public and private buildings . . . Also I can execute sculpture in marble, bronze, and clay.

Ludovico discarded Leonardo's fanciful military science. Instead he used his knowledge of anatomy and proportion to cast an immense equestrian monument that, as Leonardo claimed, 'will be to the immortal glory and eternal honour . . . of the

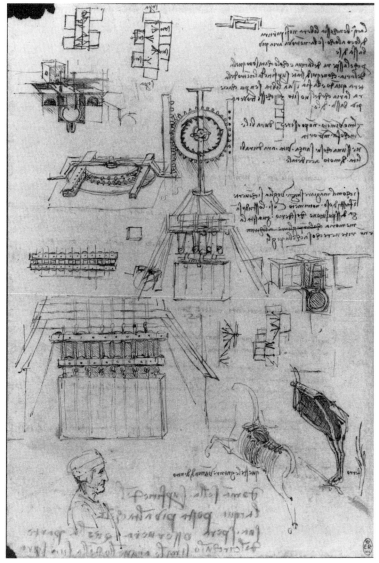

39.
Leonardo's studies
for a casting pit for
the Sforza horse
completed c.1498.
The design and
casting required all
Leonardo's artistic
and scientific
abilities, but the
statue was still
never finished.

illustrious house of Sforza'. Leonardo's sketches of the proportions and casting of the horse reveal that he used all his skill in hydraulics, anatomy, and design to envisage a statue for the civic glorification of the Sforza (Fig. 39).

Like most of his technically ambitious projects, Leonardo's horse was never built. He moved on and by 1504 he was in negotiations with the Ottoman Sultan Bayezid II to build a 350-metre bridge over the Bosphorus. 'I will erect it high as an arch', Leonardo wrote to Bayezid, 'so that a ship under full sail could sail underneath it'. Exasperated at Leonardo's unrealistic designs, Bayezid dropped him and opened equally frustrating negotiations with Michelangelo. Leonardo's great miscalculation was not committing his ideas to print in his lifetime. As a result, unlike Dürer, Leonardo left no concrete innovations to posterity. He remained a brilliant but enigmatic failure until being rescued from obscurity by Walter Pater in the 19th century.

Natural Philosophy

There was no divide between science, philosophy, and magic in the 15th century. All three came under the general heading of 'natural philosophy'. Central to the development of natural philosophy was the recovery of classical authors, most importantly the work of Aristotle and Plato. At the beginning of the 15th century Aristotle remained the basis for all scholastic speculation on philosophy and science. Kept alive in the highly influential Arabic translations and commentaries of Averroës (Plate 4) and Avicenna, Aristotle provided a systematic and 'rational' perspective on mankind's relationship with the natural world. Surviving texts like his *Physics*, *Metaphysics*, and *Meteorology* provided

scholars with the logical tools to understand the forces that created the natural world. Mankind existed within this world as a
mortal 'political animal' destined to forge social communities
thanks to his ability to reason above and beyond any other animal. From the early 15th century, humanist scholars began to
translate Aristotle into Latin and discover new texts such as the
Poetics and the pseudo-Aristotelian *Mechanics*. Engineers in
building and construction utilized the *Mechanics* with its description of motion and mechanical devices. In the civic world of
political and domestic management the Florentine humanist
Leonardo Bruni translated the *Politics, Nicomachean Ethics*, and
Oeconomicus, the latter a study of estates and household organization, which he argued were central to the civic organization of
15th-century Italian society.

As humanist scholars began to publish new translations and
commentaries on Aristotle, they also recovered a whole range of
neglected classical authors and philosophical perspectives, most
significantly exponents of Stoicism, Scepticism, Epicureanism,
and Platonism. The most decisive development was the recovery
and translation of the works of Aristotle's teacher, Plato. The
mystical, idealist Platonism of Marsilio Ficino, Nicholas of Cusa,
and Giovanni Pico della Mirandola argued that, contrary to Aristotle's belief, the soul was immortal, and aspired to a cosmic
unity and love of ultimate truth. Imprisoned in its earthly body,
the soul, according to Ficino in his *Platonic Theology* (1474), 'tries
to liken itself to God'. Ficino argued that Plato 'deemed it just and
pious that the human mind, which receives everything from God,
should give everything back to him. Thus, if we devote ourselves
to moral philosophy, he exhorts us to purify our soul so that it
may eventually become unclouded, permitting it to see the divine

light and worship of God'. This Platonic approach had two distinct advantages over Aristotelianism. Firstly, it could be accommodated much more easily into 15th-century Christian belief in the immortality of the soul and the individual's worship of God. Secondly, it defined philosophical speculation as an individual's most precious possession. Ficino's version of Platonism cleverly elevated his own profession as philosopher. Its rejection of politics in favour of mystical contemplation also suited the political philosophy of Ficino's patron, the Florentine ruler Cosimo de' Medici, who appointed Ficino as head of his Platonic Academy in 1463.

Subsequent philosophers rapidly expanded and refined Ficino's Neoplatonism. In the introduction to his 900 theological theses entitled *Conclusiones* (1486), Giovanni Pico della Mirandola claimed that in the Platonic scheme of things man is 'the maker and moulder of his own self', with the ability 'to have what he wishes, to be what he wants'. For 19th-century writers, Pico's introduction became the classic statement on the birth of Renaissance Man, and in 1882 it was given its English title, *Oration on the dignity of man*. In fact, Pico's stated aim in the *Conclusiones* was the 'concord of Plato and Aristotle', which he sought through the consultation of mystical Jewish and Arabic texts. It is our loss that, in concentrating on Pico's polemical celebration of 'man', his more inclusive attempt to unify Islamic, Jewish, and Christian theological philosophy has been mostly ignored.

Both Plato and Aristotle continued to exert an enormous influence upon the art, literature, philosophy, and science of the 16th century. Neoplatonism inspired the artistic and literary work of figures as diverse as Botticelli, Michelangelo, Erasmus, and Spenser, while Aristotelianism remained a sufficiently diverse body of work to allow scientists and philosophers to gradually revise it in line with their expanding world. However, as the century drew to a close, the intellectual primacy of both philosophers was slowly but surely being eroded. The discovery of America led Montaigne to realize in 1580 that the work of Aristotle and Plato 'cannot apply to these new lands'. Galileo's refutation of Aristotle's theories of motion, acceleration, and the nature of the universe in the early 17th century led him to conclude 'I greatly doubt that Aristotle ever tested by experiment'. Sir Francis Bacon, who complained that Aristotle 'did not consult experience', endorsed Galileo's rejection of Aristotle and began to argue the need for empirical observation in scientific analysis. By 1620 Bacon was calling for a 'Great Instauration' of learning, where 'philosophy and the sciences may no longer float in air, but rest on the solid foundation of experience of every kind, and the same well examined and weighed'. In 1626 Bacon completed his *New Atlantis*, a utopian world that drew on Plato, but whose most valued citizens were no longer philosophers but experimental scientists.

Rewriting the Renaissance

In discussing the role of the poet in his *Notebooks*, Leonardo argued:

> . . . he may be compared to those merchants at fairs who stock varied items made by different manufacturers. The poet does this when he borrows from other sciences, such as those of the orator, philosopher, cosmographer and suchlike, whose sciences are completely separate from that of the poet. Thus the poet becomes a broker, who gathers various persons together to conclude a deal.

Leonardo's literary bazaar, where the poet easily brokers the ideas of science, philosophy, diplomacy, and trade, is an appropriate metaphor for the diversity of poetry, prose, and drama that has been given the title 'Renaissance literature'. The term is as misleading and anachronistic as phrases like 'Renaissance humanism' and 'Renaissance science'. Petrarch, Boccaccio, Dante, Machiavelli, More, and Bacon were politicians and diplomats whose writings have only subsequently been labelled 'Renaissance literature'. The different genres of literary expression—poetry, drama, and prose—all responded to social and political changes in a variety of ways, all of which had regionally specific manifestations. The rise of political absolutism, religious conflict, trade and exchange with newly discovered cultures, print, and vernacular languages all transformed the production, consumption, and context of literary creativity. There is a tendency today to assume that literature from Dante to Shakespeare speaks timeless truths about the human condition, and that their Renaissance world is not so far from our own modern world. The following sections suggest that this approach avoids the alien, unfamiliar qualities of the writing of the time. Literature was intimately connected to struggles over politics, trade, printing and sexuality that were highly specific to the period. An appreciation of this strangeness is the first step in attaining a better understanding of what drove the poets and dramatists of the time.

Although the Florentine Dante Alighieri's *Divine Comedy* (completed just before his death in 1321) is usually labelled a medieval poem, its influence upon 15th- and 16th-century European poetry and prose was immense. In the three books of the *Comedy* Dante is taken on a personal journey through the graphic medieval geography of Hell, Purgatory, and Paradise by his two guides, the Roman poet Virgil and Dante's beloved, Beatrice. However, as well as being a terrifyingly vivid story of Dante's quest for spiritual salvation, the *Comedy* was also a deeply political poem embedded in the struggle for power in 14th-century Florence. Dante's political activities in the city led to his expulsion in 1302, and the *Comedy* contains numerous contemporary figures from Florentine political life through which the poet argues for a particular unification of church and monarchy based on his own political perspective.

Dante's Beatrice, an archetypal inspirational but passive female lover, influenced Petrarch in his writing of *Il Canzoniere*, a collection of 365 poems written between 1327 and 1374. Petrarch drew on Dante's collection of lyrics *New Life* (c.1294) in refining the sonnet, a heavily stylized poem of 14 lines, broken down into two sections (the octave, or first eight lines, and sestet, or final six lines) with a highly specific rhyme structure. The Petrarchan sonnet idealized the female subject at the same time as it explored the emotional complexity of the poet's identity; Petrarch complained in one sonnet that 'In this state, Lady I am because of you'. This poetic style would influence courtly Renaissance culture and poetry throughout the 15th and 16th centuries. Cardinal Bembo (1470–1547), Sir Thomas Wyatt (1503–42), Joachim du Bellay (1522–60), and Pierre de Ronsard (1524–85) all translated and refined Petrarch's poetic style to suit the sexual and political requirements of the vernacular languages of Italian, English, and French. This tradition culminated in Shakespeare's sonnet sequence (c.1600) that parodied the Petrarchan convention with its famous line, 'my mistress' eyes are nothing like the sun' (Sonnet 130). This was a romantic literary tradition based on men's social and sexual expectations. It was more indebted to Vesalius and Dürer's scientific dissections of the female body than a real concern for the desires of the poet's mistress.

Most of these poets were immersed in the changing worlds of language, politics, science, and diplomacy that have been explored throughout this book. Transformations in commercial and diplomatic communication and the impact of humanist approaches to education and philology gradually affected the development of vernacular prose writing, and nowhere more decisively than in Giovanni Boccaccio's *Decameron* (1358). Boccaccio was an urbane, successful Florentine diplomat, a product of the urban commercial world of Italy at the beginning of the 14th century. His *Decameron* was written in the wake of the 'deadly pestilence' of the plague that hit Europe in 1348. His heroines are seven unmarried 'young ladies' who take refuge from plague-ridden Florence in a rural villa, where they occupy their time by telling stories. Admitting that 'without a man to guide us it rarely happens that any enterprise of ours is brought to a worthy conclusion', the women persuade three handsome young men to accompany them. The scene is set for what sounds more like the plot of a pornographic film than a piece of innovative literary fiction.

The *Decameron* was the 14th-century equivalent of popular erotica. It played on its reader's anticipation of sexual intrigue between a group of young men and women locked away in a villa over ten nights telling each other 100 stories describing 'a variety of love adventures'. The ensuing stories of unfaithful wives, randy priests, cross-dressing women, masturbating nuns, sodomy, and impotence suggest that this was literate, urbane titillation aimed at both sexes, but controlled by a male voice.

Boccaccio concludes the *Decameron* with the anecdote that 'I was told by a lady, a neighbour of mine, that I had the sweetest tongue in the world'. The double entendre is obvious. Sex and writing are conflated, and the witty, educated elite man controls both.

Boccaccio inherited the structure of his book from Hebrew, Arabic, and Persian cycles of stories that passed into Europe from the time of the Crusades, including the Sanskrit *Panchatantra* (*c*.AD 500), and this easy literary and material commerce with the east pervades the world of the *Decameron*. Jewish and Muslim merchants, Sultans and Kings of Egypt, Turkey and Tunis all mix with Italians and are brought together in the courts and bazaars of Cairo, Alexandria, Sousse, Acre, and Armenia. His stories did not take place in churches or classrooms, but in a cosmopolitan, mercantile world that valued wit and resourcefulness in both the bedroom and the marketplace above anything else. Unlike the classical, courtly poetry of Dante and Petrarch, Boccaccio's worldly stories of 'the man in the street' quickly found a new audience of readers from the middle strata of European social life.

Kidnapping language: women respond

While the poetry of Petrarch celebrated women as idealized but silent paragons of chaste virtue, prose writing like Boccaccio's increasingly characterized them as sexually rapacious and domestically unreliable. However, some women did take advantage of the rapidly changing nature of humanist education and the rise of printing to question male-dominated poetic and fictional traditions. Their writing suggests that many of the assumptions about relations between the sexes were more actively contested than the predominantly male literary canon has led us to believe.

In the early 15th century Christine de Pizan had already adapted the Platonic tradition of the philosophical dialogue between two or more people in *The Book of the City of Ladies*, explicitly written to counter the misogyny of contemporary male writers. Throughout the 16th century a range of women writers appropriated Platonic and Petrarchan conventions to question male assumptions about women and to try to define their own personal and creative autonomy. In her *Rymes* (published posthumously in Lyons in 1545), Pernette du Guillet used Neoplatonic ideas and Petrarchan conventions to establish poetic equality with her male lover: 'just as I am yours / (And want to be), you are entirely mine' she claims in one poem, while elsewhere she attacks the fickleness and inequality of Petrarchan sentiment, assuring her female audience, 'Let's not be surprised / If our desires change'. This rejection of male poetic convention was taken even further by Louise Labé, whose poetic *Euvres* were also published in Lyons in 1555. Labé was the wife of a ropemaker, and her humble origins, combined with her desire to create a poetic voice that united male and female attributes, led many humanists and religious leaders like Calvin to castigate her as a cross-dressing prostitute. Labé used the Petrarchan sonnet to boldly criticize its objectification of women's bodies, turning the tables by asking 'What height makes a man worthy of admiration?' Rather than establishing her subservience to a fictionalized male lover, Labé competes with him, claiming in another reversal of Petrarchan convention 'I'd use the power of my eyes so well . . . That in no time I'd conquer him completely'.

This sexual frankness was combined with an insistence upon

women's right to educational attainment and creative freedom. In the 1560s Isabella Whitney established herself as a professional writer in Elizabethan England, publishing *The Copy of a Letter* (1567) and *A Sweet Nosegay* (1573), which as well as brilliantly evoking the changing urban landscape of London, also asserted some independence from the limitations of domestic life, arguing that 'til some household cares me tie, / My books and pen I will apply'. One poet who freed herself from the domestic limitations explored by Whitney was the Venetian courtesan Veronica Franco. *Rime*, her collection of poems published in 1575, both demystified the idealism of Petrarchan love from the perspective of a paid courtesan and argued that 'When we women, too, are armed and trained / We'll be able to stand up to any man'.

Writers such as Marguerite de Navarre responded to the ways in which prose fiction like Boccaccio's *Decameron* assumed women's sexual recklessness and domestic unreliability. Marguerite was the sister of King Francis I, a politically active member of the court, and an enthusiastic patron of poets and Protestants like Jean Calvin. She clashed with orthodox Catholic theologians who censured her own religious writings in the 1540s. Marguerite's cycle of 72 short stories, the *Heptameron* (1558), was closely modelled on Boccaccio's *Decameron*. Marguerite used her stories and characters to criticize men's assumptions about women's unreliability. One of her female characters argues that one man 'who's just asked me to tell the next story has, by telling a true story about *one* wretched woman, succeeded in casting a slur on *all* women'. For every story told by a man cataloguing women's sexual infidelity and duplicity, Marguerite counters with a story of women's skill and constancy in the face of male rape, abduction, and abandonment. Negotiating their relationship to the increasing religious persecution and political upheaval of mid-16th century Europe, writers like Marguerite and Isabella Whitney adapted male literary traditions to present a very different perspective on the nature of women.

Printed tales

Writers like Labé and Whitney were able to take advantage of the relatively new medium of print to establish their distinctive literary voices. Print transformed literary expression, as it created demand amongst an increasingly literate and predominantly urban audience. In France and England political authorities suppressed public religious drama such as morality and mystery plays, which had either fallen out of favour with the rise of Protestantism, or were still seen as dangerously public expressions of mass, popular sentiment. More generally, people were looking for new literary forms to understand their changing world. In 1554 the Domenican friar Matteo Bandello published his *Novelle*, short stories of contemporary urban life that, according to their author, 'do not deal with connected history but are rather a miscellany of diverse happenings'. Giambattista Giraldi, more popularly known as Cinthio, printed another collection of equally influential novellas in 1565. The prologue to his *Hecatommithi* draws on the traumatic sack of Rome in 1527. The violent events are described in terms reminiscent of the tragic Roman dramatist Seneca, and Cinthio and Bandello's stories inspired some of the greatest and bloodiest tragedies performed on the Elizabethan and Jacobean stage, including Kyd's *Spanish Tragedy* (c.1587), Shakespeare's *Othello* (1603), and Webster's *The White Devil* (*c.*1613). Like prose writing, the development of the theatre, particularly in England, was increasingly based on investment and profit rather than religious piety, a situation that allowed for increasingly complex and naturalistic representations of society and the individual.

The flexibility of the printing process also allowed writers like François Rabelais the opportunity to respond to criticism of his books and to insert contemporary events into later editions of his work. Rabelais published *Pantagruel* (1532) and *Gargantua* (1534), which recounted the comical adventures of two giants, Gargantua and his son Pantagruel. Rabelais used the adventures of his giants to satirize and parody everything from the church to the new humanist learning.

Writing in a fantastic style that mixed learned languages with vernacular French, Rabelais's description of Pantagruel captures his abundant mixing of styles. Born to a mother 'who died in childbirth' because 'he was so amazingly large and so heavy that he could not come into the world without suffocating [her]', the young giant eats whole sheep and bears, causes a scholar to shit himself, and studies the new learning in a bewildering variety of newly printed books including *The Art of Farting* and *The Chimney-Sweep of Astrology*. Pantagruel also resolves a legal dispute between the Lords Kissmyarse and Suckfart and, in a parody of seaborne discovery and scientific innovation, he finally sails away to 'the port of Utopia'.

The four books of Gargantua and Pantagruel's adventures published in Rabelais's lifetime were enormously successful, with an estimated 100,000 copies in circulation by 1600. In his prologue to *Pantagruel* Rabelais boasted, 'more copies of it have been sold by the printers in two months than there will be of the

Bible in nine years'. From 1533 the scholastics of the Sorbonne in Paris, who had been mercilessly satirized by Rabelais, took their revenge by condemning all his books as obscene and blasphemous. This provided Rabelais with the romantic aura of a persecuted but populist man of learning. His publications were banned for the rest of his life. The story of his work shows how Renaissance literary careers were often built as much on how they were advertised and distributed as on what the author wrote.

Epic failures

Rabelais's career took place against the backdrop of the intensification of political rivalry between the empires of Francis I, Charles V, Henry VIII, John III, and Süleyman the Magnificent. These claims to imperial power shaped the style of another literary genre that changed decisively in the Renaissance—the imperial epic. Ludovico Ariosto, Luís de Camões, and Edmund Spenser all produced epic poems written in the vernacular that celebrated their imperial patrons.

Ludovico Ariosto was an ambassador to one of the greatest Italian dynasties of the 15th century, the Este of Ferrara. In the opening of his epic poem *Orlando Furioso* (1516) Ariosto announces, 'I sing of knights and ladies, of love and arms, of courtly chivalry, of courageous deeds—all from the time when the Moors crossed the sea from Africa and wrought havoc in France.' This was a backward-looking, chivalric poem about 8th-century conflict between the Christian knights of Emperor Charlemagne and the Saracens. Ariosto was unable to offer a more contemporary setting, precisely because Este power was in terminal decline by the beginning of the 16th century. Real imperial power was in the hands of the Hapsburg Emperor Charles V and Sultan Süleyman the Magnificent. Reading and listening to Ariosto's poem, the noblemen of Este could fantasize about defeating Turks, the latter-day equivalent of Saracens, but this was a purely aesthetic fantasy. By the 16th century, real imperial power lay outside Italy.

Luís de Camões' epic poem *The Lusiads* (1572) returned to a more immediate past, the fading glory of another European imperial power, the Portuguese Empire. Camões was a soldier and imperial administrator who composed his poem as he worked in Africa, India, and Macau in the mid-16th century. *The Lusiads* mythologized the rise of the 15th-century Portuguese Empire by focusing on the voyage of Vasco da Gama to India in 1497. The poem argued that Portugal's scientific initiatives and imperial exploits surpassed the achievements of the Greeks and the Romans. Camões sang 'of the famous Portuguese / To whom both Mars and Neptune bowed'. In fact, by the 1570s the Portuguese Empire was already in decline, and in 1580 the Spanish King Philip II annexed it as part of the expanding Hapsburg Empire. As with Ariosto, Camões' poem was already trading on past glories.

Edmund Spenser was a political administrator, like both Ariosto and Camões, but his epic creation celebrated an empire that did not even exist. Spenser wrote *The Faerie Queene* (1590–6) while enthusiastically colonizing Ireland on behalf of his English sovereign, Queen Elizabeth I, the 'Goddesse heuenly bright, / Mirrour of grace and Maiestie diuine, / Great Lady of the greatest Isle'. In deliberately archaic English Spenser turns Elizabeth into a glorious 'Faerie Queen', and reclaims St George from his eastern origins as the patron saint of England. But this was another glorious myth. By the time that Spenser completed his poem, Elizabeth was politically isolated and her only lasting colonial legacy was to have set the scene for subsequent centuries of sectarian violence in Ireland.

Back in the bazaar

It seems fitting to end this book in what was the effective origin of the European Renaissance: the marketplace or bazaar of the eastern Mediterranean. This is the setting for one of William Shakespeare's earliest plays, *The Comedy of Errors*, first performed on the commercial stage in front of an urban audience who paid for their entertainment in London in 1594. The action takes place in one day in the marketplace of Ephesus, and revolves around mistaken identity and a missing bag of money. Egeon, an old merchant from Syracuse, lands at Ephesus in search of his long-lost twin sons. However, Ephesus is in conflict with Syracuse, and the old man is condemned to die within 24 hours unless he can raise a 1,000-mark ransom. Unknown to him, one of his sons, Antipholus (also a merchant from Syracuse) arrives at the same time in Ephesus with his servant Dromio, who, like Antipholus, also happens to have an identical twin: both twins live in the town. In the subsequent confusion Antipholus of Ephesus' wife Adriana, consigned to a life indoors, nearly ends up sleeping with her husband's twin brother, and at one point bars her real husband from the household as an interloper. The comical attempts to resolve the confusion are tinged with anxiety as Egeon reflects on 'time's extremity', as the town clock counts down the hours to his execution. Ultimately, tragedy is averted, new alliances are formed, and harmony seems to be restored.

In Shakespeare's play, as in the period more generally, the eastern bazaar or marketplace is somewhere to obtain wealth and credit; it is also an exhilarating but dangerous place that can transform people. In the midst of all the hilarity of mistaken identity, Antipholus of Syracuse is anxious that he could lose both his money and his individuality in the financial, cultural, and linguistic confusion of the market. 'I greatly fear my money is not safe', he says, before worrying that he could 'lose myself' in the Renaissance bazaar of Ephesus. Antipholus of Ephesus also learns that as well as losing your credit and your name in the marketplace, you can also lose your wife if you're not careful.

Although *The Comedy of Errors* is one of Shakespeare's earliest and often most neglected plays, it set the tone for his later works, such as *The Merchant of Venice*, *Othello*, *Antony and Cleopatra*, and *The Tempest*, with their eastern settings and fascination with how money and power transform people's lives. In Shakespeare's dramatic bazaar, where commercial speculation is paramount, time is money, and women repeatedly stray from their domestic confines, the impact of Pacioli's commercial arithmetic, Dürer's woman indoors, and the development of secular, standardized clock time becomes obvious. By the end of the 16th century, Shakespeare had inherited a sophisticated scientific and literary understanding of both time and place, which allowed his audience to understand that in *The Comedy of Errors* classical Ephesus was really late 16th-century London.

This level of global awareness and cultural mobility is the direct result of Europe's abiding transactions with the east that have been central to the argument of this book. But Shakespeare's play also represents one other commercial transaction—that which takes place between the professional playwright and the paying audience. The audience's pleasure and anxiety in watching the play's confusion in the marketplace grows out of a real appreciation of the changes to personal and public life that had taken place across Europe since the early 15th century. People lived the confusion of the liquidity of money, the anxieties surrounding wealth and exotica from far-flung places, and the impact all of this had on personal and public life. But as this book has shown, this situation had been going on for centuries, as the exchanges in the marts and bazaars of the east created the conditions for the emergence of a mobile and global world that goes beyond the intellectual and geographical boundaries of the myth of the European Renaissance.

Timeline

1453	Fall of Constantinople; end of the Hundred Years War; Alberti begins Tempio Malatestiano; Donatello completes *Gattamelata*
1459	Gozzoli, *Adoration of the Magi*; building begins on Topkapi Saray Palace
1461	Accession of King Edward IV in England; beginning of the Wars of the Roses
1467	Kritovoulos of Imbros, *The History of Mehmed the Conqueror*
1474	Ficino, *Platonic Theology*
1478	Pazzi Conspiracy in Florence; Spanish Inquisition established
1481	Death of Mehmed II; accession of Bayezid II
1486	Pico, *Conclusiones*
1488	Bartolomeu Diaz rounds the Cape of Good Hope
1492	Columbus' first voyage; conquest of Granada and expulsion of the Moors; Behaim's first terrestrial globe; Bellinis begin *St Mark Preaching in Alexandria* (completed 1504–7)
1494	Treaty of Tordesillas; beginning of the Italian Wars; Luca Pacioli, *Everything about Arithmetic, Geometry and Proportion*
1498	Da Gama reaches India
1500	Cabral lands in Brazil
1501	Michelangelo begins *David* (completed 1504)
1505	Leonardo, *Mona Lisa*; Dürer in Italy
1506	Bramante begins work on St Peter's, Rome
1509	Accession of King Henry VIII in England (rules until 1553)
1511	Erasmus, *Praise of Folly*

1512	Michelangelo completes Sistine Chapel ceiling; Erasmus, *De Copia*; accession of Sultan Selim I (rules until 1520); beginning of Fifth Lateran Council (–1517)
1513	Cortes lands in Mexico; Portuguese capture Hormuz; Piri Reis world map; Machiavelli, *The Prince*
1514	Portuguese reach China
1515	Accession of King Francis I in France (rules until 1547)
1516	Charles V becomes king of Spain, elected Holy Roman Emperor in 1519; Erasmus' first edition of the Greek *New Testament* and *Education of a Christian Prince*; More, *Utopia*; Ariosto, *Orlando Furioso*
1517	Luther's 95 theses
1520	Accession of Sultan Süleyman the Magnificent (rules until 1566)
1521	Diet of Worms; Magellan's expedition reaches the Pacific (returns 1522)
1524	Peasant's Revolt in Germany; Raphael workshop completes *Donation of Constantine*
1525	Battle of Pavia; Dürer, *A Course in the Art of Measurement*
1526	Ottoman victory over the Hungarians at the Battle of Mohács
1527	Sack of Rome
1529	Treaty of Saragossa; Diogo Ribeiro world map; Süleyman the Magnificent withdraws from siege of Vienna; German princes 'protest' against condemnation of Luther
1532	Rabelais, *Pantagruel*

1533	Henry VIII's split with Rome; Holbein, *The Ambassadors*, Regiomontanus, *On Triangles*
1536	Franco-Ottoman alliance against Hapsburgs
1543	Copernicus, *De revolutionibus*; Vesalius' *Fabrica*; Portuguese reach Japan
1545	Council of Trent begins (ends 1563)
1547	Battle of Mühlberg
1548	Titian, *Charles V at the Battle of Mühlberg*
1550	Vasari, *Lives of the Artists*
1554	Bandello, *Novelle*
1555	Peace of Augsburg, between Catholics and Lutherans; Pope Paul IV's anti-Jewish papal bull; Labé, *Euvres*
1556	Abdication of Charles V; Philip II becomes king of Spain; Tartaglia, *A General Treatise on Numbers and Measurement*; Agricola, *De re metallica*
1558	Accession of Queen Elizabeth I in England; Marguerite de Navarre, *Heptameron*
1565	Cinthio, *Hecatommithi*
1566	Accession of Sultan Selim II (rules until 1574)
1567	Whitney, *The Copy of a Letter*
1569	Mercator's world map
1570	Elizabeth I excommunicated; Ortelius, *Theatrum orbis terrarum*
1571	Defeat of Ottoman naval forces at the Battle of Lepanto
1572	St Bartholomew's Day Massacre; beginning of Protestant revolts in Netherlands; Camões, *The Lusiads*
1573	Whitney, *A Sweet Nosegay*; Vasari, *Massacre of Coligny*
1574	Accession of Murat III (rules until 1595)

1575	Franco, *Rime*
1580	Montaigne, *Essays*
1582	Introduction of the Gregorian Calendar
1590	Spenser, *The Faerie Queene*, Books I–III; Sidney, *Arcadia*; Marlowe, *The Jew of Malta*
1594	Shakespeare, *The Comedy of Errors*
1600	English East India Company founded
1601	Shakespeare, *Hamlet*
1603	Shakespeare, *Othello*; death of Elizabeth I; accession of James I
1605	Bacon, *Advancement of Learning*

FURTHER READING

Introduction

JACOB BURCKHARDT, *The Civilisation of the Renaissance in Italy*, tr. S. G. C. Middlemore (London, 1990)

W. K. FERGUSON, *The Renaissance in Historical Thought: Five Centuries of Interpretation* (New York, 1970)

STEPHEN GREENBLATT, *Renaissance Self-Fashioning: From More to Shakespeare* (Chicago, 1980)

MARY S. HERVEY, *Holbein's Ambassadors, the Picture and the Men: An Historical Study* (London, 1900)

WALTER MIGNOLO, *The Darker Side of the Renaissance* (Ann Arbor, Mich., 1995)

ERWIN PANOFSKY, *Studies in Iconology: Humanist Themes in the Art of the Renaissance* (Oxford, 1939)

1. A global Renaissance

EZIO BASSANI and WILLIAM FAGG, *Africa and the Renaissance* (New York, 1988)

JERRY BROTTON and LISA JARDINE, *Global Interests: Renaissance Art between East and West* (London, 2000)

CHARLES BURNETT and ANNA CONTADINI (EDS.), *Islam and the Italian Renaissance* (London, 1999)

DEBORAH HOWARD, *Venice and the East* (New Haven, Conn., 2000)

HALIL INALCIK, *The Ottoman Empire: The Classical Age 1300–1600*, tr. Colin Imber and Norman Itzkowitz (New York, 1973)

GÜLRU NECIPOĞLU, 'Süleyman the Magnificent and the representation of power in the context of Ottoman–Hapsburg–Papal rivalry', *Art Bulletin* 71 (1989), 401–27

JULIAN RABY, *Venice, Dürer and the Oriental Mode* (London, 1982)

2. The humanist script

ELIZABETH EISENSTEIN, *The Printing Press as an Agent of Change*, 2 vols. (Cambridge, 1979)

LUCIAN FEBVRE, *The Coming of the Book*, tr. David Gerard (London, 1976)

ANTHONY GRAFTON and LISA JARDINE, *From Humanism to the Humanities: Education and the Liberal Arts in Fifteenth- and Sixteenth-Century Europe* (London, 1986)

WILLIAM IVINS, *Prints and Visual Communications* (Cambridge, Mass., 1953)

ADRIAN JOHNS, *The Nature of the Book: Print and Knowledge in the Making* (Chicago, 1998)

JILL KRAYE (ED.), *The Cambridge Companion to Renaissance Humanism* (Cambridge, 1996)

3. Church and state

JOHN BOSSY, *Christianity in the West, 1400–1700* (Oxford, 1985)

THOMAS BRADY ET AL. (EDS.), *Handbook of European History, 1400–1600*, Vol. I (Leiden, 1994)

EUAN CAMERON, *The European Reformation* (Oxford, 1991)

DAVID M. LUEBKE (ED.), *The Counter-Reformation* (Oxford, 1999)

STEVEN OZMENT, *The Age of Reform, 1250–1550* (New Haven, Conn., 1980)

EUGENE RICE, *The Foundations of Early Modern Europe*, rev. edn. (New York, 1993)

4. Putting things into perspective

MICHAEL BAXANDALL, *Painting and Experience in Fifteenth-Century Italy* (Oxford, 1972)

JERRY BROTTON and LISA JARDINE, *Global Interests: Renaissance Art between East and West* (London, 2000)

ALISON COLE, *Art of the Italian Renaissance Courts* (London, 1995)

JILL DUNKERTON ET AL., *From Giotto to Dürer* (London, 1991)

CRAIG HARBISON, *The Art of the Northern Renaissance* (London, 1995)

EVELYN WELCH, *Art in Renaissance Italy 1350–1500* (Oxford, 1997)

5. Brave new worlds

JERRY BROTTON, *Trading Territories: Mapping the Early Modern World* (London, 1997)

MARY BAINES CAMPBELL, *Wonder and Science* (New York, 1999)

TONY GRAFTON, *New Worlds, Ancient Texts* (New York, 1995)

JAY LEVENSON (ED.), *Circa 1492: Art in the Age of Exploration* (Washington, 1992)

J. H. PARRY, *The Age of Reconnaissance* (London, 1963)

JOAN PAU RUBIÉS, *Travel and Ethnology in the Renaissance* (London, 2000)

6. Experiments, dreams, and performances

MARIE BOAS, *The Scientific Renaissance 1450–1630* (London, 1962)

WALTER COHEN, *Drama of a Nation* (New York, 1985)

BRIAN COPENHAVER and CHARLES B. SCHMITT, *Renaissance Philosophy* (Oxford, 1992)

MARGARET FERGUSON ET AL. (EDS.), *Rewriting the Renaissance* (Chicago, 1986)

STEPHEN GREENBLATT, *Renaissance Self-Fashioning: From More to Shakespeare* (Chicago, 1980)

ANN ROSALIND JONES, *The Currency of Eros: Women's Love Lyric in Europe, 1540–1620* (Bloomington, 1990)

DAVID QUINT, *Epic and Empire* (Princeton, 1993)

NANCY SIRAISI, *Medieval and Early Renaissance Medicine* (Chicago, 1990)

Index